Downsizing Federal Government Spending

ISBN 978-1-944424-74-9 (print)
eISBN 978-1-944424-75-6

Cato Institute
1000 Massachusetts Ave., N.W.
Washington, D.C. 20001
www.cato.org

Contents

INTRODUCTION   1

 1. Cutting Federal Spending   3
 2. Agricultural Policy   13
 3. K-12 Education   19
 4. Higher Education   29
 5. Medicaid   39
 6. Medicare   51
 7. Social Security   61
 8. Military Budget   73
 9. Foreign Aid   85
10. Earned Income Tax Credit   97
11. Infrastructure Investment   103
12. Fiscal Federalism   111
13. Special-Interest Spending   119
14. Fiscal Rules that Work   127
15. Averting National Bankruptcy   135

CONTRIBUTORS   141

Introduction

On the campaign trail, presidential candidate Donald Trump complained about "waste, fraud, and abuse all over the place" in the federal government. He promised that if elected, "We will cut so much, your head will spin." He highlighted the threat posed by federal debt, and said "we are going to cut many of the agencies, we will balance our budget."

Since assuming office, Trump has proposed both increases and cuts to spending. The president's initial budget document, released in March, includes $54 billion in spending cuts to offset a proposed defense spending increase. The cuts would affect a broad range of agencies and would be a good start for the major downsizing effort we need in Washington.

Following the budget release, the administration in April introduced a "Comprehensive Plan for Reforming the Federal Government and Reducing the Federal Civilian Workforce." The plan launches a year-long effort by the president's budget office and federal agencies to come up a large package of specific budget cuts. The package will be included in the fiscal year 2019 budget.

The April plan tasks federal agencies with identifying programs and activities that are nonessential, that violate federalism, and that would flunk a cost-benefit test. Agencies should propose eliminating or restructuring activities that do not pass muster with these and other criteria.

Cato Institute scholars have proposed major cuts to the federal budget, and this e-book assembles new essays by our experts on cutting spending and reforming programs in agriculture, defense, education, foreign aid, health care, infrastructure, aid to the states, Social Security, and other activities.

It remains to be seen whether the Trump administration will sustain its initial efforts at spending restraint, and whether Congress will go along with proposed reductions. Economic circumstances will likely keep the pressure on policymakers to make reforms. Current deficits of more than half a trillion dollars are expected to rise to more than a trillion by 2023.

Growing spending and debt are undermining economic growth and may push the nation into a financial crisis in coming years.

Federal spending cuts would help avert a crisis, while spurring economic growth by shifting resources from lower-valued government activities to higher-valued private ones. The federal government has expanded into many areas that should be left to state and local governments, businesses, charities, and individuals. That expansion is sucking the life out of the private economy and creating a top-down bureaucratic society. Cutting spending programs and related regulations would expand freedom by giving people more control over their lives.

Further analysis of the programs covered in this e-book, and analysis of other federal spending activities, is available at www.Cato.org and www.DownsizingGovernment.org.

Chris Edwards
Cato Institute
August 2017

1. Cutting Federal Spending

Federal government spending is rising, deficits are chronic, and accumulated debt is reaching dangerous levels. Growing spending and debt are undermining economic growth and may push the nation into a financial crisis in coming years. The solution to these problems is to downsize every federal department by cutting the most harmful and unneeded programs. This chapter proposes specific cuts that would balance the budget and reduce projected spending by almost one-quarter within a decade.

Over recent decades, the federal government has expanded into many areas that should be left to state and local governments, businesses, charities, and individuals. That expansion is sucking the life out of the private economy and creating a top-down bureaucratic society that is alien to American traditions.

Federal spending cuts would revive growth by shifting resources from lower-valued government activities to higher-valued private ones. Cuts would also enhance civil liberties by dispersing power away from Washington. And cuts would help reduce the number of costly regulations that are imposed as part of spending programs.

The Congressional Budget Office (CBO) projects that federal spending will rise from 20.7 percent of gross domestic product (GDP) this year to 23.4 percent by 2027 under current law. Over the same period, tax revenues will rise more modestly, reaching 18.4 percent of GDP in 2027. As a consequence, rising spending will produce increasingly large deficits.

Policymakers should change course. They should cut spending and eliminate deficits. The plan presented here would balance the budget over time and generate growing surpluses. Spending would be reduced to 18.0 percent of GDP by 2027, or almost one-quarter less than the CBO projection for that year.

Some economists claim that cutting government spending would hurt the economy, but that notion is based on faulty Keynesian theories. In fact, spending cuts would shift resources from often mismanaged and damaging government programs to more productive private activities, thus

3

Figure 1.1
Projected Federal Revenues and Spending
Percent of GDP

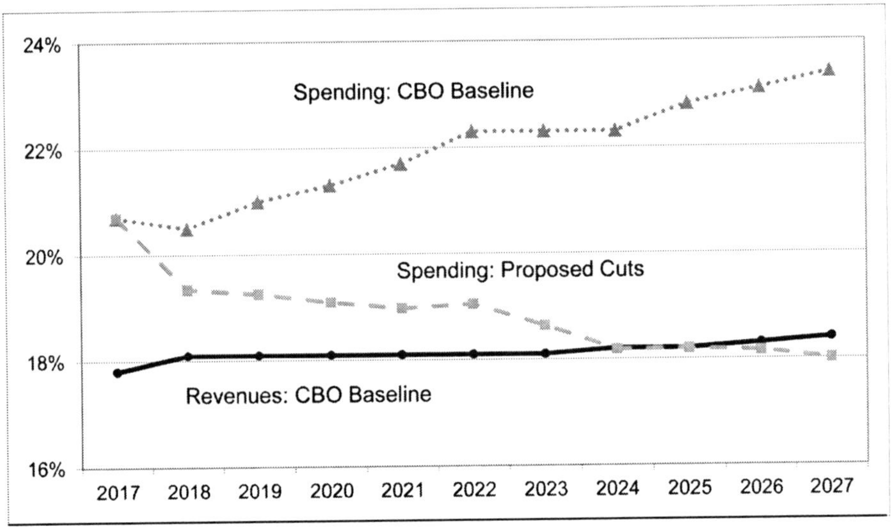

SOURCE: Author's calculations.

increasing overall GDP. Markets have mechanisms to allocate resources to high-value activities, but the government has no such capabilities.

It is true that private businesses make many mistakes, but entrepreneurs and competition are constantly fixing them. By contrast, federal agencies follow failed and obsolete approaches decade after decade. That is why moving resources out of the government would be a net gain for the overall economy.

Policymakers should not think of spending cuts as a necessary evil to reduce deficits. Rather, the federal government's fiscal mess is an opportunity to implement reforms that would spur growth and expand freedom. The plan proposed here includes a menu of possible spending reforms. These and other reforms are discussed further at DownsizingGovern ment.org.

Spending Cut Overview

The starting point for a spending cut plan is the CBO's baseline budget projections. Figure 1.1 shows CBO projections from January 2017 for revenues (solid line) and spending (dotted line) as a percentage of GDP. The gap between the two lines is the federal deficit, which is expected to grow steadily without reforms.

4

The dashed line shows projected spending under the reform plan proposed here. Under the plan, spending would decline from 20.7 percent of GDP in 2017 to 18.0 percent by 2027. The deficit would be eliminated by 2024, and growing surpluses would be generated after that. Spending cuts would be phased in over 10 years and would total $1.5 trillion annually by 2027, including reduced interest costs.

Falling spending and deficits would create budget room for tax reforms. One reform would be to repeal the tax increases under the 2010 Affordable Care Act. Another reform would be to slash the federal corporate tax rate from 35 percent to 15 percent to match the federal rate in our largest trading partner, Canada. Such a cut would spur stronger growth, boost worker wages as businesses increased investment, and lose little revenue over the long term.

Spending Cut Details

Tables 1.1 and 1.2 list proposed cuts to reduce federal spending to 18.0 percent of GDP by 2027. Table 1.1 shows cuts for health care and Social Security. Those reforms would be implemented right away, but the value of savings would grow over time. The figures shown are the estimated annual savings by 2027, generally based on CBO projections.

Table 1.2 shows cuts to programs other than health care and Social Security. These cuts would be valued at $499 billion in 2017, but the plan assumes that they would be phased in one-tenth each year over the next decade.

The reforms listed in Tables 1.1 and 1.2 are deeper than the savings from "duplication" and "waste" often mentioned by policymakers. We should cut hundreds of billions of dollars of "meat" from federal departments, not just the obvious "fat." If the activities that are cut are useful to society, then state governments or private groups should fund them, and they would be more efficient doing so than the federal government.

The proposed cuts to subsidies, aid to the states, military spending, and entitlement programs are discussed below. The final section discusses the privatization of federal activities. Further analyses of these and other cuts are at DownsizingGovernment.org.

Subsidies to Individuals and Businesses

The federal government funds about 2,300 subsidy programs, more than twice as many as in the 1980s, according to my analysis of the

5

Table 1.1
Proposed Federal Budget Cuts:
Health Care and Social Security

Agency and Activity	Annual Savings $billions, 2027
Health Care	
Repeal Affordable Care Act exchange subsidies	106
Repeal Affordable Care Act Medicaid expansion	142
Block grant Medicaid and grow at 2%	119
Increase Medicare premiums	69
Increase Medicare cost sharing	10
Cut Medicare improper payments by 50%	77
Cut non-Medicaid state health grants by 50%	43
Total cuts	**566**
Social Security Administration	
Price index initial Social Security benefits	27
Raise the normal retirement age for Social Security	10
Cut Social Security Disability Insurance by 25%	54
Cut Supplemental Security Income by 25%	19
Total cuts	**110**
Total annual spending cuts in 2027	**$676**

SOURCE: Author's calculations.

Catalog of Federal Domestic Assistance. The *scope* of federal activities has expanded in recent decades along with the *size* of the federal budget. The federal government subsidizes farming, health care, school lunches, rural utilities, the energy industry, rental housing, aviation, passenger rail, public broadcasting, job training, foreign aid, urban transit, and many other activities.

Each subsidy causes damage to the economy through the required taxation. And each subsidy generates a bureaucracy, spawns lobby groups, and encourages even more people to demand government handouts. Individuals, businesses, and nonprofit groups that become hooked on federal subsidies essentially become tools of the state. They lose their independence, have less incentive to work and innovate, and shy away from criticizing the government.

Table 1.2
Proposed Federal Budget Cuts
Discretionary Programs and Other Entitlements

Agency and Activity	Annual Savings $billions, 2017
Department of Agriculture	
End farm subsidies	27.8
Cut food subsidies by 50%	51.0
End rural subsidies	3.9
Total cuts	**82.7**
Department of Commerce	
End telecom subsidies	1.2
End economic development subsidies	0.2
Total cuts	**1.4**
Department of Defense	
End overseas contingency operations	65.0
Total cuts	**65.0**
Department of Education	
End K-12 education grants	23.7
End all other programs	88.1
Total cuts (terminate the department)	**111.8**
Department of Energy	
End subsidies for renewables	1.7
End fossil/nuclear/electricity subsidies	1.7
Privatize power marketing administrations	0.5
Total cuts	**3.9**
Department of Homeland Security	
Privatize TSA airport screening	5.9
Devolve FEMA activities to the states	12.0
Total cuts	**17.9**
Department of Housing and Urban Development	
End rental assistance	30.9
End community development subsidies	10.2
End public housing subsidies	6.5
"Other cuts"	9.2
Total cuts (terminate the department)	**56.8**

(continued)

Table 1.2
(continued)

Agency and Activity	Annual Savings $billions, 2017
Department of the Interior	
Reduce net outlays by 50% through spending cuts, privatization, and user charges	6.8
Total cuts	**6.8**
Department of Justice	
End state/local grants	6.2
Total cuts	**6.2**
Department of Labor	
End employment and training services	3.7
End Job Corps	1.6
End trade adjustment assistance	0.6
End Community Service for Seniors	0.4
Total cuts	**6.3**
Department of Transportation	
Cut highway/transit grants to balance trust fund	12.2
Privatize air traffic control (federal fund savings)	2.2
Privatize Amtrak and end rail subsidies	4.5
Total cuts	**18.9**
Department of the Treasury	
Cut earned income tax credit by 50%	30.5
End refundable part of child tax credit	20.1
End refundable part of Am. Opp. Tax Credit	4.0
Total cuts	**54.6**
Other Savings	
Cut foreign aid by 50%	13.2
Cut federal civilian compensation costs by 10%	32.9
Privatize the Army Corps of Engineers (Civil Works)	6.9
Privatize the Tennessee Valley Authority	0.4
Privatize the U.S. Postal Service	n/a
Repeal Davis-Bacon labor rules	9.0
End EPA state/local grants	4.3
Total cuts	**66.7**
Total annual spending cuts	**$499.0**

SOURCE: Author's calculations.

Table 1.2 includes cuts to subsidies in agriculture, commerce, energy, housing, foreign aid, and other activities. Those cuts would not eliminate all of the unjustified subsidies in the budget, but they would be a good start. Government subsidies are like an addictive drug, undermining America's traditions of individual reliance, voluntary charity, and entrepreneurialism.

Aid to the States

Under the Constitution, the federal government was assigned specific limited powers, and most government functions were left to the states. Unfortunately, policymakers and the courts have mainly discarded constitutional federalism in recent decades. Through "grants-in-aid" Congress has undertaken many activities that were traditionally reserved to state and local governments. Grant programs are subsidies that are combined with federal regulatory controls to micromanage state and local activities. Federal aid to the states totals about $700 billion a year and is distributed through more than 1,100 separate programs.

The theory behind grants-in-aid is that the federal government can operate programs in the national interest to efficiently solve local problems. However, the aid system does not work that way in practice. Most federal politicians are preoccupied by the competitive scramble to maximize subsidies for their states, and they generally ignore program efficiency and overall budget limitations.

Furthermore, federal aid stimulates overspending by state governments and creates a web of complex federal regulations that undermine state innovation. At all levels of the aid system, the focus is on spending and regulatory compliance, not on delivering quality public services. The aid system destroys government accountability because each level of government blames the other levels when programs fail. It is a triumph of expenditure without responsibility.

The grants-in-aid system is a roundabout funding system for state and local activities. It serves no important economic purpose, and it should be eliminated. Tables 1.1 and 1.2 include cuts to state grants for education, health care, highways, justice, transit, and other activities. There is no reason why such activities should not be funded by state and local governments or the private sector.

Military Spending

Cato Institute defense experts Christopher Preble and Benjamin Friedman have proposed numerous cuts to U.S. military spending (see

Chapter 8). They argue that the United States would be better off taking a wait-and-see approach to distant threats, while letting friendly nations bear more of the costs of their own defenses. They note that U.S. policymakers support many extraneous missions for the military aside from the basic role of defending the nation.

As such, the military budget should be cut in a prudent fashion as part of an overall plan to downsize the government and balance the budget. The plan proposed here assumes that spending on overseas contingency operations—which will be $65 billion in 2017—would be reduced to zero over time.

Medicare, Medicaid, and Social Security

The projected growth in Medicare, Medicaid, and Social Security is the main cause of America's looming fiscal crisis. Budget experts generally agree on the need to restructure these programs, and Table 1.1 includes a variety of reforms.

Policymakers should repeal the 2010 Affordable Care Act. That would reduce spending on Medicaid and end spending on the exchange subsidies. In addition, policymakers should convert Medicaid from an open-ended matching grant to a block grant, while giving state governments more program flexibility. That was the successful approach used for welfare reform in 1996, which encouraged state innovation.

Table 1.1 includes modest Medicare changes based on CBO estimates. Reforms include increasing deductibles and increasing premiums for Part B to cover 35 percent of the program's costs. It also assumes that the Medicare improper payment rate would be cut in half.

However, larger Medicare reforms are needed than just these cuts. Cato scholars have proposed moving to a system based on individual vouchers, personal savings, and consumer choice for elderly health care (see Chapter 6). Such a reform would create incentives for patients to become more discriminating consumers of health services and providers to improve system quality and reduce costs.

For Social Security, initial benefits should be indexed to prices rather than wages to slow the program's growth. The plan also includes a CBO option to modestly raise the normal retirement age. In addition, the fraud-plagued Social Security Disability Insurance and Supplemental Security Income programs would be trimmed 25 percent compared with current spending projections.

10

In addition to these reforms, Social Security should be transitioned to a system of private accounts, as discussed in Chapter 7. Private accounts would increase fairness, boost personal financial security, and improve work incentives by partly converting payroll taxes into contributions to accounts that are personally owned.

Privatization

A privatization revolution has swept the world since the 1980s. Following Britain's lead, governments in more than 100 countries have transferred thousands of state-owned businesses to the private sector. More than $3 trillion of railroads, energy companies, postal services, airports, and other businesses have been privatized.

Privatization helps spur economic growth. It allows entrepreneurs and markets to reduce costs, improve service quality, and increase innovation. It also benefits the environment by reducing the wasteful use of resources.

Despite the global success of privatization, reforms have largely bypassed our own federal government. Many activities that have been privatized abroad remain in government hands in this country. U.S. policymakers should learn from foreign privatization and enact proven reforms here.

Table 1.2 includes the privatization of Amtrak, the air traffic control system, airport screening, electric utilities, the Army Corps of Engineers, and the U.S. Postal Service. Such reforms would reduce budget deficits and improve management, as described in related chapters and at Downsizing Government.org.

Conclusions

CBO's long-term baseline projections show that federal spending and debt will rise continuously in coming years as a share of GDP, which will undermine economic growth and cause a serious financial crisis at some point. The sooner that policymakers tackle major spending reforms, the better to avoid accumulating even more debt. Leaders of numerous other nations have pursued vigorous cost cutting when their spending and debt started getting out of control. There is no reason why our political leaders cannot do the same.

Suggested Readings

Cato Institute. www.DownsizingGovernment.org.
Congressional Budget Office. "Options for Reducing the Deficit: 2017 to 2026." December 8, 2016.

————. "The Budget and Economic Outlook: 2017 to 2027." January 24, 2017.

Edwards, Chris. "Fiscal Federalism." DownsizingGovernment.org, Cato Institute, June 2013.

————. "Options for Federal Privatization and Reform Lessons from Abroad." Cato Institute Policy Analysis no. 794, June 28, 2016.

————. "Washington's Largest Monument: Government Debt." Cato Institute Tax & Budget Bulletin no. 71, September 8, 2015.

————. "Why the Federal Government Fails," Cato Institute Policy Analysis no. 777, July 27, 2015.

General Services Administration. Catalog of Federal Domestic Assistance. Washington: Government Printing Office, various editions.

—Prepared by Chris Edwards

2. Agricultural Policy

The U.S. Department of Agriculture (USDA) spends $25 billion or more a year on subsidies for farm businesses. The particular amount each year depends on the market prices of crops, the level of disaster payments, and other factors. Most agricultural subsidies go to farmers of a handful of major crops, including wheat, corn, soybeans, and cotton. Roughly a million farmers and landowners receive federal subsidies, but the payments are heavily tilted toward the largest producers.

Some farm subsidy programs counter adverse fluctuations in prices, revenues, and production. Other programs subsidize farmers' conservation activities, insurance coverage, product marketing, export sales, research and development, and other activities. Agriculture is no riskier than many other industries, yet the government has created a uniquely large welfare system for farmers.

In 1996, Congress enacted some pro-market reforms under the "Freedom to Farm" law. The law allowed farmers greater flexibility in planting and moved toward reliance on market supply and demand. But Congress reversed course in the late 1990s and passed a series of supplemental farm subsidy bills. As a result, subsidies that were expected to cost $47 billion over the seven years of the 1996 law ended up costing $121 billion. In 2002, Congress enacted a farm bill that further reversed the 1996 reforms. The law increased projected subsidy payments, added new crops to the subsidy rolls, and created a new price guarantee scheme called the "countercyclical" program. In 2008, Congress overrode a presidential veto to enact farm legislation that added further subsidies. The law created a permanent disaster program and added a revenue protection program for farmers to lock in profits from high commodity prices. It added a sugar-to-ethanol program to help keep sugar prices artificially high, and it added new subsidies for "specialty crops" such as fruits and vegetables.

In 2014, Congress passed yet another huge farm bill. The bill changed the structure of subsidies but did not cut the overall level of benefits. The law ended the direct payment program, the countercyclical program, and the Average Crop Revenue Election program. However, it expanded the largest farm subsidy program—crop insurance—and added two new subsidy programs, the Agricultural Risk Coverage (ARC) program and the Price Loss Coverage (PLC) program. When the 2014 farm bill was passed, supporters claimed that it would save taxpayer money, but the opposite has happened. The Congressional Budget Office now estimates that the ARC and PLC programs will cost billions of dollars a year more than originally promised. The cost of crop insurance is also rising.

All of these subsidies ensure that farm incomes are much higher than the incomes of most other Americans. Farm programs are welfare for the well-to-do, and they induce overproduction, inflate land prices, and harm the environment. They should be ended, and American farmers should stand on their own two feet in the marketplace.

Eight Types of Farm Subsidy

1. Insurance. Crop insurance run by the USDA's Risk Management Agency has become the largest farm program, with annual outlays of about $8 billion. Subsidized insurance protects against various business risks, such as adverse weather, low production, and low revenues. It covers more than 100 crops, but corn, cotton, soybeans, and wheat are the main ones. It subsidizes both insurance premiums and the administrative costs of the 19 private insurance companies that offer policies to farmers. The companies receive the subsidies and earn excess profits from the high premiums they charge; but farmers also benefit because the USDA pays about 60 percent of their premium costs, according to the Government Accountability Office (GAO). Indeed, economist Bruce Babcock finds that most farmers make money on insurance over time, receiving more in claims payouts than they pay in premiums. Congress channels the largest portion of farm subsidies through the insurance program to obscure the identities of the wealthy recipients. Under prior farm programs, news stories often identified the millionaires receiving farm subsidies, which was embarrassing to Congress. Insurance subsidies are less transparent and have no income limits, and so Congress has expanded the program over the years.

2. Agricultural Risk Coverage (ARC). This program pays subsidies to farmers if their revenue per acre, or alternatively their county's revenue per acre, falls below a benchmark or guaranteed amount. Generally, the lower the prices and revenues are, then the larger the subsidies paid out are. More than 20 crops are covered, from wheat and corn to chickpeas and mustard. ARC subsidies fluctuate, but they were about $7 billion in 2016.

3. Price Loss Coverage (PLC).

This program pays subsidies to farmers based on the average national price of each particular crop compared with the crop's reference price. The larger the fall in a crop's price below its reference price, the larger the payout to farmers. PLC subsidies also cover more than 20 crops. PLC subsidies fluctuate, but they were about $2 billion in 2016.

4. Conservation programs.

The USDA runs many farm conservation programs, which cost taxpayers more than $5 billion a year. The largest is the Conservation Reserve Program, which pays farmers about $1.7 billion a year to keep millions of acres of their land out of production.

5. Marketing loans.

This program was created during the New Deal. The original idea was to give farmers a loan at harvest time so that they could hold their crops to sell at a higher price later on. But the program has evolved into just another subsidy program that delivers higher payments to farmers when market prices are low. These subsidies cost about $400 million in 2016.

6. Disaster aid.

The government operates various disaster aid programs for many types of farmers, from wheat growers, to livestock producers, to tree fruit producers. In addition to permanent disaster programs, Congress sometimes distributes additional aid after adverse events. Disaster and supplemental aid costs about $1 billion to $2 billion a year.

7. Marketing and export promotion.

The Agriculture Marketing Service spends about $1.2 billion a year on farm and food promotion activities. The Foreign Agricultural Service spends about $1.4 billion a year on a range of activities, including marketing U.S. farm and food products abroad through 93 foreign offices.

8. Research and other support.

Most American industries fund their own research and development, but the government employs thousands of scientists and other experts to aid the agriculture industry. The USDA spends about $3 billion a year on agriculture and food research at more than 100 locations. The department also provides many other services, such as loan programs for farmers, statistical services, and economic studies.

Six Reasons to Repeal Farm Subsidies

1. Subsidies redistribute wealth upward. Farm subsidies transfer the earnings of taxpayers to well-off farm businesses and landowners. USDA data show that farm incomes have soared far above average U.S. incomes. In 2015, the average income of farm households was $119,880, which was 51 percent higher than the $79,263 average of all U.S. households. The same year, the median income of farm households was $76,735, which was 36 percent higher than the U.S. median of $56,516.

Although farm programs are advertised as support for small farmers, most subsidies go to the largest farms. Economist Vincent Smith found that the largest 15 percent of farm businesses receive more than 85 percent of all farm subsidies. Over the years, many well-known billionaires have received farm subsidies because they are the owners of farmland. Prior to the 2014 farm bill, the Environmental Working Group (EWG) found that 50 people on the Forbes 400 list of the wealthiest Americans received farm subsidies. The new farm bill channels the largest share of subsidies through insurance companies, making it hard to determine the identities of recipients. But in 2015, the GAO found that at least four recipients of crop insurance subsidies have a net worth of more than $1.5 billion.

2. Subsidies damage the economy. The extent of federal coddling and micromanagement of the agriculture industry is unique. In most industries, market prices balance supply and demand, profits steer investment, businesses take risks, and entrepreneurs innovate to improve quality and reduce costs. Those market mechanisms are blunted and undermined in U.S. agriculture, causing a range of economic harms, including overproduction, distorted land use, distorted choice of crops, inflated land prices, and inadequate cost control.

3. Subsidies are prone to scandal. Like all government subsidy programs, farm programs are subject to both bureaucratic waste and recipient fraud. One problem is that some farm subsidies are paid improperly as farmers create business structures to get around legal subsidy limits. Another problem is that Congress and the USDA distribute disaster payments in a careless manner, with payments going to farmers who do not need them. The EWG found another boondoggle: the "prevented planting" program covers losses if conditions during a season prevent farmers from planting some areas. EWG found that billions of dollars over the years have been paid to farmers who would not normally have planted the areas included in their USDA claims.

4. Subsidies undermine U.S. trade relations. Global stability and U.S. security are enhanced when less developed countries achieve economic growth. America can help by encouraging poor nations to adopt free markets and expand their international trade. However, U.S. and European farm subsidies and agricultural import barriers undermine progress on achieving open trading relationships. Federal sugar protections block freer trade within the Americas, for example, while enriching sugar growers and harming U.S. consumers and U.S. food companies that use sugar.

5. Subsidies harm the environment. Federal farm policies damage the natural environment in numerous ways. For example, subsidies cause overproduction, which draws lower-quality farmlands into active production. As a result, areas that might otherwise have been used for parks, forests, grasslands, and wetlands get locked into less efficient agricultural use. Subsidies are also thought to induce excessive use of fertilizers and pesticides. Producers on marginal lands that have poorer soils and climates tend to use more fertilizers and pesticides, which can cause water contamination problems. Sugar cane production has expanded in Florida because of the federal sugar program, for example, and the phosphorous in fertilizers used by the growers causes damage to the Everglades.

6. Agriculture would thrive without subsidies. If U.S. farm subsidies were ended and agricultural markets deregulated, farming would change. Different crops would be planted, land usage would change, and some farm businesses would contract while others would expand. But a stronger and more innovative industry would emerge with greater resilience to market fluctuations. Private insurance, other financial tools, and diversification would help cover risks, as they do in other industries.

An interesting example of farmers prospering without subsidies is New Zealand. In 1984, New Zealand ended its farm subsidies, which was a bold stroke because the country is four times more dependent on farming than is the United States. The changes were initially met with resistance, but New Zealand farm productivity, profitability, and output have soared since the reforms. New Zealand farmers cut costs, diversified land use, sought nonfarm income, and developed niche markets such as kiwi fruit. The Federated Farmers of New Zealand argues that that nation's experience "thoroughly debunked the myth that the farming sector cannot prosper without government subsidies." That myth needs to be debunked in the United States as well.

Suggested Readings

Babcock, Bruce A. *Crop Insurance: A Lottery That's a Sure Bet*. Washington: Environmental Working Group, February 2016.

Cato Institute. "Department of Agriculture." DownsizingGovernment.org.

Coleman, Robert. "The Rich Get Richer: 50 Billionaires Got Federal Farm Subsidies." Environmental Working Group *AgMag*, April 18, 2016.

Cox, Craig, Soren Rundquist, and Anne Weir. *Boondoggle: "Prevented Planting" Insurance Plows Up Wetlands, Wastes $Billions*. Washington: Environmental Working Group, April 28, 2015.

Environmental Working Group. "Key Issues: Farming." *AgMag*.

Government Accountability Office. "Crop Insurance: Reducing Subsidies for Highest Income Participants Could Save Federal Dollars with Minimal Effect on the Program." GAO-15-356, March 2015.

———. "Farmers Have Been Eligible for Multiple Programs and Further Efforts Could Help Prevent Duplicative Payments." GAO-14-428, July 2014,

O'Neil, Colin. "Are Billionaires Getting Crop Insurance Subsidies?" Environmental Working Group *AgMag*, April 28, 2016.

Smith, Vincent H. "Cash Crop." *Washington Examiner*, May 11, 2015.

———. "Crony Farmers." *U.S. News & World Report*, January 14, 2016.

———. "A Midterm Review of the 2014 Farm Bill." American Enterprise Institute, February 10, 2016.

U.S. Department of Agriculture, Economic Research Service. Various data on farm incomes and subsidy payments.

—Prepared by Chris Edwards

3. K–12 Education

The Constitution gives the federal government no authority to exercise control over elementary and secondary education, including by spending money and attaching conditions to the funds, the primary mode by which Washington has influenced education. And no, the Founders did not exclude dominion over education from the specific, enumerated powers given to Washington because they thought such authority was subsumed under the "general welfare" clause. They did not include it because education at the time was believed best left in the hands of parents and civil society—the families and communities closest to the children—and certainly not in a distant, national government. Fifty years of experience with major and, until very recently, constantly expanding federal meddling in K–12 education has proven them right.

A Brief History of Federal Involvement

The federal government, relatively speaking, is a newcomer to elementary and secondary schooling. As many advocates of a federal role in education are quick to point out, the Land Ordinance of 1785 and Northwest Ordinance of 1787 did contain provisions calling for territories to dedicate the revenue coming from the sale of portions of land to educational purposes. But those laws preceded the Constitution, were often ignored, and asserted no federal control over what might be taught, how, or by whom. And clearly, James Madison, one of the primary architects of the Constitution, as well as other members of Congress, did not consider education to be among the matters rightfully within the reach of the federal government. In 1792, Madison argued against a bill to provide aid to fisheries by noting that were Congress to decide that the Constitution furnished the authority to spend money on fisheries, they could also, absurdly, "take into their own hands the education of children." Indeed, as recently as 1943, the U.S. Constitution Sesquicentennial Commission, chaired by President Franklin Delano Roosevelt, published a document that included the following: "Q. Where, in the

Constitution, is there mention of education? A. There is none; education is a matter reserved for the states."

Thus, federal governance of elementary and secondary education is of relatively recent vintage. A U.S. Department of Education was created in 1867, but it was downgraded to a bureau two years later and was charged mainly with collecting statistics, not governing. Not until the Soviet Union sent the satellite Sputnik into orbit in 1957, and the American public briefly panicked, did the federal government for the first time try to exercise significant influence over education. That foray, the National Defense Education Act, primarily aimed to improve capacity in science and engineering at the college level. And the act maintained a clear connection to a constitutionally explicit federal responsibility: providing for the common defense.

Only in the mid-1960s, under President Lyndon Johnson's "Great Society," did Washington completely break with the Constitution by enacting a K–12 law untethered to national defense. The Elementary and Secondary Education Act (ESEA) was enacted in 1965 and sought, primarily, to provide "compensatory" funding to districts serving low-income populations. The intent was not to exercise authority over states and districts, but to equalize resources. What was discovered over the course of about two decades, however, was that funding alone made little difference in outcomes.

By the early 1980s, many people considered the American education system to be failing. As a result, the federal role began to morph from one focused on funding, to one focused on control—control made possible only by attaching coercive rules to federal dollars. Indeed, the Reagan administration at first strove to eliminate the cabinet-level U.S. Department of Education, which had just been re-created in 1979. But in 1983, the administration published *A Nation at Risk*, a report with a Sputnik-like effect. It intoned, "If an unfriendly foreign power had attempted to impose on America the mediocre educational performance that exists today, we might well have viewed it as an act of war." The administration's second education secretary, William Bennett, became a major personality to whom the media and public looked for guidance on education issues, and the 1988 reauthorization of the ESEA for the first time called on states and districts to demonstrate academic achievement. The era of "standards and accountability" had begun, and it arguably reached its apex with the 2002 ESEA reauthorization, the No Child Left Behind Act (NCLB).

NCLB asserted enormous control over the shape and functioning of K–12 education, requiring that all schools adhere to uniform state standards, be held accountable by aligned standardized tests, and bring all students (including numerous subsets based on race and other group identities) to full "proficiency" by the end of the 2013–2014 school year. Schools were punished if any group failed to make "adequate yearly progress" toward that full-proficiency goal.

Over time, parents and others increasingly came to dislike the law's strictures and huge emphasis on standardized tests, and irritation evolved into disgust with the "Race to the Top" program. Among other things, that program in effect required states to use the so-called Common Core national curriculum standards and to use one of just two federally funded, Common Core–aligned tests, to compete for a share of a $4 billion pool of funding. The program also called for greater data collection on students and for teacher evaluations based on students' standardized test scores. In addition, the Obama administration started to offer NCLB waivers in exchange for states adopting administration-selected policies. Those centralizing efforts united opposition on the left and right against Washington, the new "national school board."

The end result of exhaustion with federal control is the latest iteration of the ESEA, the Every Student Succeeds Act (ESSA), which President Barack Obama signed in December 2015. The ESSA is intended to remove the most onerous provisions of NCLB, Race to the Top, and NCLB waivers; those provisions include the mechanistic "adequate yearly progress," coercion to adopt the Common Core, and use of standardized test scores in teacher evaluations. It is also supposed to eliminate much of the unilateral authority the secretary of education had under the Race to the Top and waiver systems. Still, a note of caution is needed: as of May 2017, the Department of Education was drafting ESSA regulations after Congress scrapped Obama administration accountability rules, and the administration did not try to complete spending regulations. The Trump administration appears more inclined to give states latitude, but the executive branch could still gut legislative intent on such matters as funding equity and measuring academic performance.

Outcomes

What have we gotten from ballooning federal spending and control? First of all, it is very difficult—perhaps impossible—to fully separate the effects of federal policy from numerous other variables that affect

21

academic achievement. Those variables include state policies, local policies, students' family lives, and attitudes toward education. Thus, we cannot say definitively that federal policy caused something to happen or not happen. Nevertheless, the evidence strongly suggests that federal K–12 interventions have been largely ineffectual and almost certainly not worth the money expended on them. Note that "governance" does not include interventions by federal courts, most notably in *Brown v. Board of Education*, which have often been necessary to enforce the Fourteenth Amendment's equal protection requirements against state and district discrimination.

Historically, the evidence is powerful that neither government provision of schools nor compulsory attendance was needed for most people to educate their children. Numerous historians have noted that white Americans (blacks were often prohibited by law from receiving an education) had very high rates of literacy before there was significant provision of "common schools"; and very large percentages of Americans were sending their children to school before there were compulsory attendance laws. People valued education and did not appear to need government provision, which largely followed widespread education.

To assess learning in the modern era, the most consistent, national measure we have is the National Assessment of Educational Progress (NAEP) Long-Term Trend Assessment. The assessment is a federal test given to a nationally representative sample of students—but without stakes attached and, thus, insulated against "gaming"—which has remained largely consistent since the 1970s. What does it show? Looking at 17-year-olds over the decades, achievement is almost completely flat, even though—as Figure 3.1 shows—the inflation-adjusted expenditure on the average student's education has nearly *tripled*. That trend has been largely echoed by SAT scores; after controlling for numerous variables including self-selection of test takers, we see that those scores have also stagnated. We can also look at federal expenditures per pupil. As Figure 3.2 illustrates, inflation-adjusted federal spending per student rose from $443 in the 1969–1970 academic year to $1,148 in 2012–2013, again a near-tripling.

What do we see on NAEP during the No Child Left Behind period? It is difficult to pick a starting date for the NCLB period. The law was enacted in early 2002, but NAEP long-term trend exams were given in 1999 and 2004—neither very close to NCLB's first year. That said, both reading and math scores for 17-year-olds were slightly lower in 2012— the last time the exam was given—than in 1999 (the exam was also altered

Figure 3.1
Change in NAEP Long-Term Trend Results (17-Year-Olds) vs. Change in Total Spending for a Child's K–12 Education, in 2014 dollars, by Graduation Year, 1970–2012

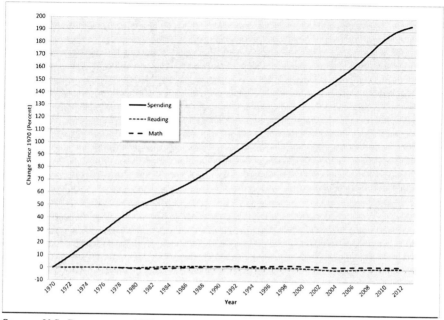

SOURCE: U.S. Department of Education, National Center for Education Statistics, *Digest of Education Statistics, 2015*, Table 236.55, https://nces.ed.gov/programs/digest/d15/tables /dt15_236.55.asp?current=yes (Missing data linearly interpolated); U.S. Department of Education, National Center for Educational Statistics, National Assessment of Educational Progress, http://nces.ed.gov/nationsreportcard/.

in 2004, somewhat affecting comparability). We can also look at the "main" NAEP (more frequent exams given since the 1990s that are not necessarily meant to remain comparable over time) to get a sense of NCLB trends. Those are also disappointing, with average reading scores for 12th graders dropping slightly between 1998 and 2015 (Figure 3.3). Math scores are available only between 2005 and 2015, so they do not provide a pre-NCLB benchmark to try to discern the law's impact; scores increased slightly in that brief period (Figure 3.4).

National test scores for high school seniors have essentially not budged despite huge spending increases. That said, scores for younger students and some subgroups such as African Americans did improve over the NCLB period. The improvement occurred mainly at the beginning, which could reflect more a new emphasis on standardized testing—including

23

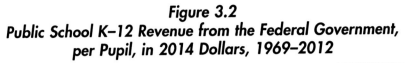

Figure 3.2
Public School K–12 Revenue from the Federal Government,
per Pupil, in 2014 Dollars, 1969–2012

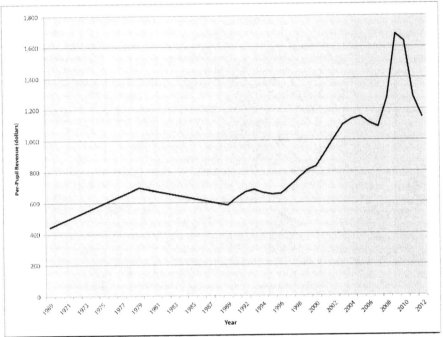

SOURCE: U.S. Department of Education, National Center for Education Statistics, *Digest of Education Statistics, 2015,* Table 235.10.

testing strategies—than significantly improved learning. Meanwhile, some research that has tried to isolate the effects of NCLB has detected some possible benefit, but usually small and restricted to one subject. That is not bad news, but it hardly overrides the evidence that, in the final analysis, learning does not appear to have improved overall.

Recommendations

Perhaps as a result of the relatively poor outcomes indicated by standardized tests and, more likely, because of the public's broad rejection of education heavily focused on such tests, Congress determined that federal power in education should be reduced. The recently enacted ESSA is supposed to return much authority to the states. Senate education committee chair Lamar Alexander (R-TN) hailed it as "a dramatic change in direction for federal education policy," reversing "the trend toward what had become, in effect, a national school board." However, as the regulations

Figure 3.3
Main NAEP Reading Scores (17-Year-Olds), 1992–2015

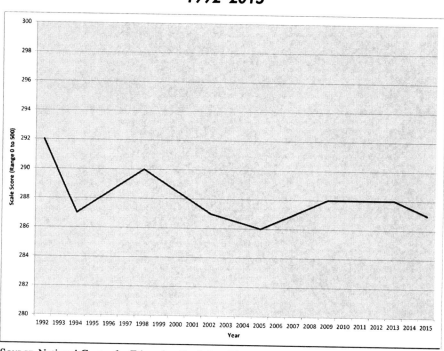

SOURCE: National Center for Education Statistics, *The Nation's Report Card: 2015 Mathematics and Reading at Grade 12,* http://www.nationsreportcard.gov/reading_math_g12_2015/#.

are being drafted and debated, there is a very real danger that they will depart from the intent of the law and retain much federal control over standards, tests, and accountability systems. That must not be allowed to happen. Indeed, even if reforms based on "accountability" are effective, they originated in states such as Texas and North Carolina, and federal officials mainly observed those and decided they liked the idea. Then, instead of letting "laboratories of democracy" work, they imposed the model on all states, at the very least creating a national backlash against such policies, and perhaps dampening enthusiasm even in states that would have been inclined to adopt the approach on their own.

Ending the hyper-prescriptiveness of NCLB is only the start of what Congress should do. Ultimately, federal involvement in education should be eliminated, with the following exceptions: (1) enforcing the Fourteenth Amendment in states or districts that clearly discriminate against different groups in their provision of education; (2) exercising the federal govern-

Figure 3.4
Main NAEP Math Scores (17-Year-Olds), 2005–2015

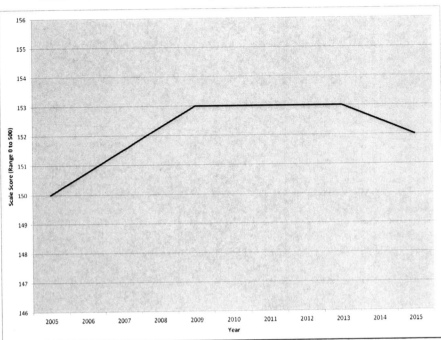

Source: National Center for Education Statistics, *The Nation's Report Card: 2015 Mathematics and Reading at Grade 12*, http://www.nationsreportcard.gov/reading_math_g12_2015/#.

ment's fully constitutional authority over the District of Columbia and education on military bases; (3) continuing "impact aid" for districts with federal installations (that cannot be taxed) and the large concentrations of federally connected children those installations bring there, and (4) working to improve education on Native American reservations. Even those four exceptions call for a light touch. The Department of Education's Office of Civil Rights has been too aggressive in declaring matters such as transgender bathroom access a federal concern when the nation has had little chance to contemplate and discuss the competing values—especially equality and privacy—at stake; it is generally best for the people of Washington, D.C., to exercise control over their own education system; and impact aid may well be too high and wasted.

One final concern is worth noting: empowering parents to choose educational options for their children is a powerful thing, enabling the people who know their children best to select their learning environments, and people with different norms and desires to avoid zero-sum battles.

But that does not mean it is desirable for Washington to "voucherize" federal education spending, including with tax credits for paying private school tuition or donating to groups that give scholarships. Federal school choice—except for the D.C. Opportunity Scholarship Program, for military dependents, and for children on Native American reservations—would be unconstitutional. Just as important, it would create a very real danger of imposing national regulations over such things as standards and testing, ultimately rendering private schools nearly as homogenous as public. The motives behind such proposals as "Pell Grants for Kids" are good, but the dangers are too great.

Conclusion

The Constitution does not grant the federal government any authority to govern education, and for most of our history Washington stayed out. Over the past few decades, unfortunately, that changed—first with funding, then with control. Pinpointing the effect—or lack thereof—of federal intervention on education is difficult. But the evidence strongly suggests that, while Washington has driven no lasting improvements, it has marginalized and angered parents and other citizens. The federal government should drop the reins and let people at the state level decide where and how to exercise education authority.

Suggested Readings

Alger, Vicki E. *Failure: The Federal Misedukation of America's Children.* Oakland, CA: Independent Institute, 2016.

Arons, Stephen. *Short Route to Chaos: Conscience, Community, and the Re-Constitution of American Schooling.* Amherst, MA: University of Massachusetts Press, 1997.

Coulson, Andrew J. *Market Education: The Unknown History.* New Brunswick, NJ: Transaction Books, 1999.

———. "State Education Trends: Academic Performance and Spending over the Past 40 Years." Cato Institute Policy Analysis no. 746, March 18, 2014.

Glenn, Charles L. *The Myth of the Common School.* Amherst, MA: University of Massachusetts Press, 1987.

McCluskey, Neal P. *Feds in the Classroom: How Big Government Corrupts, Cripples, and Compromises American Education.* Lanham, MD: Rowman & Littlefield, 2007.

Tooley, James. *The Beautiful Tree: A Personal Journey into How the World's Poorest People Are Educating Themselves.* Washington, DC: Cato Institute, 2009.

—*Prepared by Neal McCluskey*

4. Higher Education

In *Universities in the Marketplace*, former Harvard president Derek Bok observes, "Universities share one characteristic with compulsive gamblers and exiled royalty: there is never enough money to satisfy their desires." This chapter explores the harmful effects of federal involvement in higher education, especially distortions wrought by feeding colleges' insatiable financial cravings. When considered in conjunction with the Tenth Amendment dictum that "the powers not delegated to the United States by the Constitution . . . are reserved to the States respectively, or to the people," the message is clear: the federal government should withdraw from higher education.

Student Debt and Financial Aid: Where Are We Now?

The Great Recession brought with it a new focus on student debt and the price of college, issues made especially visible by three things: (1) in 2010, total student loan debt surpassed total credit card debt for the first time; (2) the 2011 Occupy Wall Street protests focused to a significant extent on college costs; and (3) in 2012, total student debt broke the psychologically huge $1 trillion mark. As a result, we have seen significant attention paid to the cost of college and to proposals by major presidential candidates that the federal government incentivize states to spend more on their institutions of higher learning and make tuition either debt free or totally free.

This attention has come in the midst of significant expansions and reforms in federal student aid programs. For the past several decades, the federal government has been the primary provider of aid to students, through grants, loans, work study, and tax incentives for higher education expenditures. Since 2007, that role has grown significantly larger. The Bush and Obama administrations and Congress raised the maximum Pell Grant and expanded the percentage of students eligible for it, increased the maximum amounts available through loans, offered loan forgiveness for people who work for government or eligible nonprofit entities, introduced income-based repayment that caps payments at 10 or 15 percent of adjusted gross income and forgives remaining debt after 20 or 25 years, and cut interest rates on student loans.

Washington also changed how it finances loans, eliminating the "guaranteed" loan program in which borrowers obtained loans from ostensibly private lenders, but the federal government essentially guaranteed lenders a profit with the backing of federal dollars. That program was replaced with lending direct from the federal treasury. Finally, the Obama administration proposed creating a federal database on outcomes for every institution enrolling students with federal aid—almost every college—and eventually rating schools using measures such as graduation and loan-repayment rates. Facing major opposition from schools and policymakers over the rating idea, the administration eventually created the "College Scorecard," which enables users to find outcomes for first-time, full-time students 10 years after they enrolled at—but did not necessarily graduate from— a school.

Federal Aid: Seems Good, Is Probably Bad

A growing body of empirical literature strongly suggests that much federal financial aid does not translate into greater affordability for students. Instead, it has such unintended effects as these: institutions replacing their own aid dollars, state legislators decreasing direct subsidies, and just plain tuition inflation. In 1987, Secretary of Education William Bennett famously surmised that federal aid was encouraging tuition inflation. In a *New York Times* op-ed titled "Our Greedy Colleges," he wrote that "federal student aid policies do not cause college price inflation, but there is little doubt that they help make it possible." Essentially, when we give people money to pay for something, we give the providers the incentive to raise their prices.

Colleges are revenue maximizers. They can always think of something they could do with more money: start new programs, pay employees more, avoid cost-saving changes such as eliminating underutilized programs, build new fitness facilities or even a water park. Even economists Robert Archibald and David Feldman, who largely disagree with the "Bennett Hypothesis," tacitly concede this point in their book *Why Does College Cost So Much?* They argue that anything that might constrain colleges would at least appear to compromise "quality," which they seem to define as supplying everything someone might say is good, including not just

Top Five College Water Parks

1. University of Missouri "Tiger Grotto": According to the Mizzou website, "The Grotto will transform your dullest day into a vacation, with our resort quality facilities and atmosphere that will unwind you, even with the most stressful of schedules. The Grotto features a zero-depth pool entry with a high-powered vortex, lazy river and waterfall. Our hot tub, sauna and steam room will help you loosen up after a hard workout."
2. Texas Tech "Student Leisure Pool": According to Texas Tech's website, this is "the largest leisure pool on a college campus in the United States." It features, among other things, a 645-foot long, lazy river and a 25-person hot tub.
3. University of Alabama: According to the school's "University Recreation" webpage, the outdoor pool facility features, among other things, a "current channel," "spray features," a "tanning shelf," a "water slide," and a "bubble bench."
4. Missouri State: The school's pool features LED lights that change color at night, a 16-seat spa and sauna near the pool, and a 20-yard zip line.
5. Louisiana State University (under construction): The $84 million aquatics facility will feature a 536-foot lighted lazy river in the shape of "LSU," two "bubbler lounges," and a 21,000-square-foot sun deck made of "broom finished concrete with sand blasted etching of tiger stripes."

small classes, but also "research or public service" and limited adjunct professors.

Figure 4.1 illustrates that over roughly the last quarter century, inflation-adjusted aid per full-time-equivalent student has increased at a remarkable rate, nearly tripling. That increase has almost certainly abetted the doubling of inflation-adjusted tuition, fees, and room and board charges at public four-year institutions, as well as the roughly 75 percent increase in prices at four-year private schools. Of course, aid is not the only factor in college pricing. Skeptics of the Bennett Hypothesis often blame cuts in direct state and local subsidies to colleges as the primary culprit behind rising prices. But those cuts do not meaningfully affect private institutions, which receive very little in direct state and local subsidization. Plus, public

Figure 4.1
Percent Change in Aid per Full-Time-Equivalent Undergraduate Student and Published Tuition, Fees, and Room and Board Charges Since the 1990–91 Academic Year, Inflation Adjusted

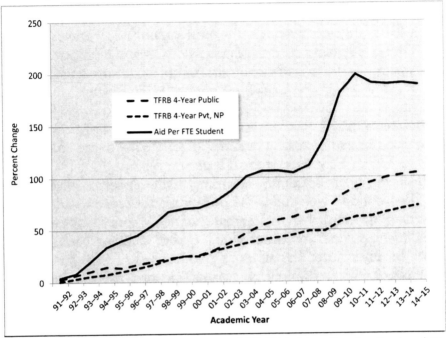

SOURCE: College Board, *Trends in College Pricing 2015*, Table 2, http://trends.collegeboard.org /college-pricing/figures-tables/tuition-and-fees-and-room-and-board-over-time-1, and *Trends in Student Aid 2015*, Table 3, http://trends.collegeboard.org/student-aid/figures-tables/average -aid-student-over-time-postsecondary-undergraduate-graduate.
NOTE: TFRB = tuition, fees, and room and board; NP = nonprofit; FTE = full-time equivalent.

institutions have actually seen an increase in total state and local funding since 1990. Where there has been an appreciable funding reduction is on a per-pupil basis, but that is primarily a consequence not of tight-fisted states, but of enrollment increasing from 7.8 million to 11.1 million full-time-equivalent students between 1990 and 2015.

The effect of aid on what students actually pay, as opposed to the "sticker price" they are ostensibly charged, is partially illustrated in Figures 4.2 (public institutions) and 4.3 (private institutions). The illustration is only "partial" because the figures exclude student loans, which—at least in theory—must be paid back. In practice, student loans are cheap because of government subsidization, and they are often eligible for some level of forgiveness. They are also awarded to many people who almost certainly

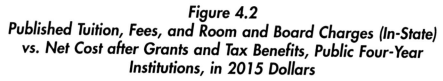

Figure 4.2
Published Tuition, Fees, and Room and Board Charges (In-State) vs. Net Cost after Grants and Tax Benefits, Public Four-Year Institutions, in 2015 Dollars

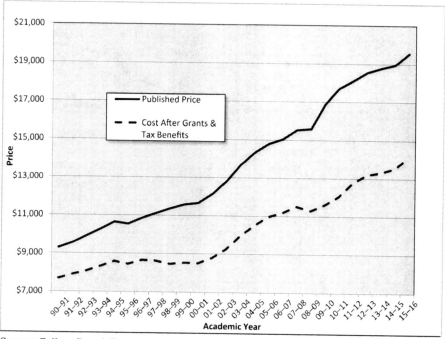

Source: College Board, *Trends in College Pricing 2015*, Table 7, https://trends.collegeboard.org /college-pricing/figures-tables/average-net-price-over-time-full-time-students-sector.

would be unable to get such loans on the private market, for both financial and academic reasons. They truly are *aid*. Of course, they also enable students to pay what schools want to charge, the central point of the Bennett Hypothesis. That said, even looking only at prices—before tax benefits and grants (including institutional dollars)—we see the effect of aid. At public four-year institutions, while the inflation-adjusted sticker price of tuition, fees, and room and board rose 110 percent between 1990 and 2015, net prices rose only 84 percent. At private, four-year institutions, published prices grew 78 percent, but net prices rose only 39 percent. Loans helped cover the remaining difference.

Federal aid clearly enables colleges to ramp up their prices. It also likely gooses student demand for programs and amenities increasingly removed from academic necessity, including gourmet food, deluxe housing, lots of recreational and entertainment programming, and even on-campus water

33

Figure 4.3
Published Tuition, Fees, and Room and Board Charges vs. Net Cost after Grants and Tax Benefits, Private Four-Year Institutions, in 2015 Dollars

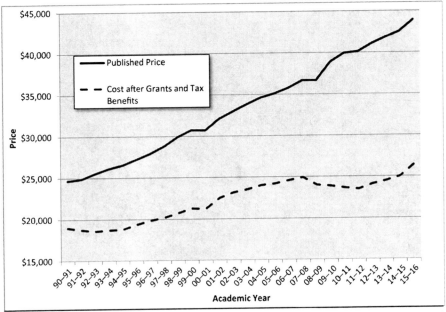

SOURCE: College Board, *Trends in College Pricing 2015*, Table 7, https://trends.collegeboard.org/college-pricing/figures-tables/average-net-price-over-time-full-time-students-sector.

parks! Indeed, researchers Brian Jacob, Brian McCall, and Kevin Stange found that for all but the top academic performers, students put more emphasis on schools' amenities than their academic offerings. That means many colleges may well be locked into an amenities "arms race" fueled, at least in part, by subsidies that incentivize students to demand lots of extras.

Perhaps this state of affairs would be tolerable if the higher education system performed magnificently, clearly imparting lots of new, crucial knowledge and skills. But much evidence suggests it does not.

First, roughly half of all students who enter college never finish. Many of those who do not finish have received aid despite being unprepared for college-level work. Thus, they often have debt but no degree with which to increase their earnings and repay what they owe. Indeed, small debtors comprise the biggest chunk of loan defaulters. The students with heftier debt levels have often gotten undergraduate degrees and gone on to graduate schools and usually earn enough to comfortably pay off their loans.

That said, even many who do finish college have difficulty finding work that requires their degree. According to a 2014 report from the Federal Reserve Bank of New York, approximately one out of every three bachelor's degree holders is in a job not requiring the credential. Meanwhile, the surfeit of degree holders is apparently leading to "credential inflation." According to research by the human resources firm Burning Glass Technologies, many job advertisements call for a degree even though the people currently occupying those positions typically do not have one, and the desired skills are not college level. Finally, while the wage premium for having a degree versus just completing high school is quite large—perhaps as much as $1 million over one's lifetime—earnings for people with at least an undergraduate degree have been essentially stagnant for roughly the last two decades.

At least people are learning a lot more, right? Perhaps not, at least according to the incomplete measures we have. Research by Richard Arum and Josipa Roksa indicates that college students reported spending 40 hours per week on academic pursuits in the early 1960s, but just 27 hours in 2011. Time spent studying declined from 25 hours per week in 1961 to 20 hours in 1980 and 13 hours in 2003. The National Assessment of Adult Literacy determined that, in 1992, about 40 percent of adults whose highest degree was a bachelor's were proficient in reading prose, but by 2003—the only other year the assessment was administered—only 31 percent were proficient. Among people with advanced degrees, prose proficiency dropped from 51 percent to 41 percent. To a large extent, a degree seems to serve as a signal of someone's basic attributes—maybe general intelligence and ability to complete a long-term task—but does not necessarily indicate someone has obtained valuable skills. Still, employers can easily demand a degree because someone else is usually paying.

The U.S. System: Don't Make It Worse

As problematic as American higher education is, it works much better than either our elementary and secondary system, or most other countries' postsecondary systems. American universities dominate world rankings; the United States is the top destination for students pursuing studies outside of their home countries; and we have by far the greatest number of top scholars, including Nobel Prize winners. Why? Because as wasteful and distorting as aid to students is, it is far better to attach money to

35

students and give institutions autonomy to govern and shape themselves than to have the government operate the schools and fund them directly. We want a system that can supply varied types of education and that allows students and schools to respond quickly to changing needs in the workforce. Freedom is much better suited to those goals than top-down control.

Of course, American higher education is far from perfect in that regard. Public colleges and universities receive heavy direct subsidies from state and local governments that render them significantly insulated from the pressures of student demands. And private, nonprofit schools often have big endowments or other sources of funds accumulated through tax-favored donations. For-profit colleges and, to a lesser extent, community colleges have often been the most responsive to changing workforce demands.

What that tells us is, first, Congress should not enact legislation that would offer federal funding to states in exchange for greatly increased subsidies to public colleges and lower or zero tuition. Although such legislation would reduce sticker prices and debt, it would render higher education even less efficient than the current system. And, of course, it would come with a hefty taxpayer price tag.

Second, Congress should cease the outsized assault we have seen on for-profit institutions over the last several years. Students who attend for-profit schools do tend to have relatively high loan default levels, and they do not earn as much as graduates of four-year public and private, non-profit schools. But for-profits work with the students with the greatest challenges—older, poorer, more likely to have families and full-time jobs—even compared with community colleges. Moreover, for-profits tend to be relatively quick to expand or create new programs when demand arises and to scale down or end programs when demand subsides. In other words, they are best at responding to changing market demands. Nevertheless, like all sectors of higher education, they have inflated prices, big noncompletion problems, and too much debt default—due, in large part, to the artificial incentives created by student aid.

Removing the Federal Government from Higher Education

James Madison wrote in *Federalist* No. 45, "The powers delegated by the proposed Constitution to the federal government are few and defined. . . . [They] will be exercised principally on external objects, as war, peace, negotiation, and foreign commerce." Since the Constitution grants the federal government no role in higher education, Washington may only be involved in ways that support legitimate federal concerns. That essentially means maintaining the Senior Reserve Officers' Training Corps, service academies, and national defense–related research. Otherwise the federal government should withdraw from higher education.

Washington cannot, however, withdraw immediately. Abruptly ending federal student aid, especially, would leave millions of students scrambling for funds and would overwhelm private lenders, schools, and charitable organizations that have made plans based on expected levels of federal involvement. What follows is an overview of a six-year plan to withdraw the federal government from higher education:

- Two years: End direct federal aid to institutions. With the exceptions of Howard University and Gallaudet University, both of which are in the District of Columbia, colleges do not typically receive direct federal subsidies of major size. If schools are to be directly subsidized, state or local governments should do it. Also, federal tax incentives, which are heavily skewed to the well-to-do—such as 529 plans, Coverdell Education Savings Accounts, and Lifetime Learning Credits—should end, though existing savings should receive the tax treatment promised when the money was deposited.
- Four years: Phase out "unsubsidized" federal loans, which are loans available without regard to financial need. There is little justification for supplying loans to people who could otherwise afford to pay for college. The maximum available loan should be reduced in equal increments over four years, to a complete phaseout.
- Six years: Eliminate all federal student aid programs. Each year after the enactment of the federal phaseout, the maximum Pell Grant should be reduced in equal increments. Similarly, maximum "subsidized" loan sizes should be reduced in equal increments.

Conclusion

The federal presence in higher education is ultimately self-defeating, fueling artificially higher prices, incentivizing overconsumption, and making it harder and more expensive for people to access the education they need. The solution is not to incentivize greater direct subsidies for the ivory tower, but to eliminate the subsidies we already have. That will help transform the currently bloated, teetering ivory tower into manageably sized educational options accessible to everyone who needs them.

Suggested Readings

Arum, Richard, and Josipa Roksa. *Academically Adrift: Limited Learning on College Campuses.* Chicago: University of Chicago Press, 2011.

Fried, Vance. "Federal Higher Education Policy and the Profitable Nonprofits." Cato Institute Policy Analysis no. 678, June 15, 2011.

Jacob, Brian, Brian McCall, and Kevin M. Stange. "College as Country Club: Do Colleges Cater to Students' Preferences for Consumption?" National Bureau of Economic Research Working Paper no. 18745, January 2013.

McCluskey, Neal P. "How Much Ivory Does This Tower Need? What We Spend on, and Get from, Higher Education." Cato Institute Policy Analysis no. 686, October 27, 2011.

———. "The Newly Updated Help-that-Hurts List." SeeThruEdu, January 7, 2016.

Pierce, Kate. "College, Country Club or Prison." *Forbes*, July 29, 2014.

Vedder, Richard. *Going Broke by Degree: Why College Costs Too Much.* Washington: American Enterprise Institute, 2004.

—Prepared by Neal McCluskey

5. Medicaid

Counterintuitively, the most important thing policymakers can do to improve access to care for the poor is not to provide direct assistance to the poor, but to liberalize the health care sector. The great virtue of a market system is that it uses innovation to fill in the cracks in the health care sector so that fewer vulnerable patients fall through. A market system drives prices for medical care and health insurance downward. It minimizes the problem of preexisting conditions by offering protection against preexisting conditions even to the uninsured. Liberalization would reduce unmet medical need by bringing health care within the reach of those who could not previously afford it, making health care of ever-increasing quality available to an ever-increasing number of people. Liberalization would make the problem of unmet need smaller and leave the rest of society wealthier, so we could better help the shrinking number of patients who still could not help themselves. Government intervention merely causes the cracks in the health care sector to widen.

Even so, no matter how well a market system improves quality and access, there will always be patients who cannot afford the medical care they need, either because they never had the resources or because they chose not to purchase health insurance. This chapter discusses how to address, in a market system, the shrinking number of patients who cannot help themselves.

The Samaritan's Dilemma

Any effort to help people in need confronts what economists call "the Samaritan's dilemma"—the idea that, just as it is possible to help too little, it is also possible to help too much. Helping too much induces people who could be self-reliant to take advantage of charitable assistance and do less to help themselves. As the assistance becomes more generous, fewer people provide for themselves. They contribute less to the economy—and to charity. Helping too much perversely *increases* the amount of "need" and the burden of charity, while simultaneously reducing society's ability to bear that larger burden.

Ideally, voluntary charity and government assistance would avoid both helping too little and helping too much. Yet there is no obvious "right" place to strike that balance. The optimal amount of charitable assistance depends on actual need, the costs of assistance and dependence, and donor preferences. All of these vary across space and time.

Some approaches are more effective than others. Voluntary charities have the incentive and the ability to ensure their resources assist only the truly needy. For example, voluntary charities can lose funding if donors learn their contributions are going to people who don't need assistance. In contrast, the government has little incentive or ability to strike an optimal balance. Politicians must craft broad eligibility rules for government programs. Typically, these take the form of a legal entitlement to benefits for anyone who meets certain criteria. When bureaucrats identify beneficiaries who technically meet those criteria, but nevertheless need no assistance, they have little ability or incentive to exclude them. On the contrary, they face incentives to provide assistance to nonneedy applicants, because their careers depend on a thriving program and beneficiaries can sue the government for withholding benefits to which they are legally entitled. Taxpayers might want to cut programs that provide assistance to nonneedy applicants but lack the freedom to withdraw their "contributions" in protest, so programs that provide assistance to nonneedy applicants rarely see their funding reduced. Thus, government welfare programs tend to err on the side of subsidizing lots of people who don't need assistance.

Instances in which government appears to help too much abound.

- In 2004, budget constraints led Missouri to cut more than 100,000 people from its Medicaid rolls. Though the share of low-income children enrolled in Medicaid fell from 50 percent to 40 percent, one study found that "increases in other types of insurance coverage prevented an increase in the share that were uninsured." Before the Patient Protection and Affordable Care Act (ACA) was implemented, Medicaid-eligibility expansions in Arizona, Delaware, Maine, and Oregon did not reduce those states' uninsured rates. They were accompanied by declines in private coverage.
- A study of Medicaid expansions by ACA supporters projected "high rates of crowd-out for Medicaid expansions aimed at working adults (82 percent), suggesting that the Medicaid expansion provisions of

[the ACA] will shift workers and their families from private to public insurance without reducing the number of uninsured very much."

- Economist Casey Mulligan found that the ACA creates larger disincentives to work than any law Congress has enacted in 70 years. In some cases, workers find that working more leaves them with *lower* incomes.

The most important thing that policymakers can do to help the poor obtain health insurance and medical care is adopt policies that spur cost-saving innovations and lower prices. Falling prices do not involve a Samaritan's dilemma. Welfare traps the poor in poverty; falling prices help them climb out. The government can help the poor most of all by reforming Medicare (see Chapter 6) and the tax treatment of health care, and by deregulating medicine and health insurance.

In addition, federal and state governments operate three main programs to provide medical care to low-income Americans: Medicaid, the State Children's Health Insurance Program, and premium subsidies available through the Patient Protection and Affordable Care Act's health insurance "exchanges." Congress should repeal or drastically reform each of these programs.

Medicaid

Medicaid is an almost $600 billion program that exists ostensibly to provide health care to the poor. The federal government jointly administers Medicaid with state and territorial governments. States that wish to participate in Medicaid must pay a portion of the cost of a federally mandated set of health benefits to a federally mandated population of eligible individuals. In return, each state receives matching federal funds to administer its program. The federal treasury matches *any* amount a state spends on its Medicaid program. States receive unlimited matching funds when they make their Medicaid benefits more comprehensive or extend eligibility to more people than the federal government requires. Overall, the federal government currently finances between 63 percent and 65 percent of Medicaid spending.

All states participate in the traditional Medicaid program, which primarily serves four low-income groups: mothers and their children, the disabled, the elderly, and those needing long-term care. Specific eligibility criteria vary by state. Historically, 57 percent of traditional Medicaid funding has come from the federal government and 43 percent has come from the states.

The ACA gives states the option to expand their Medicaid programs to all adults with incomes below 138 percent of the federal poverty level

($16,394 for single adults in 2016). The principal beneficiaries are able-bodied adults. The federal government pays 100 percent of the cost of the ACA's Medicaid expansion from 2014 through 2016. The federal share then phases down to 90 percent by 2020. Thirty-one states have implemented the ACA's Medicaid expansion.

For beneficiaries, Medicaid is an entitlement. So long as they meet the eligibility criteria, they have a legally enforceable claim to benefits. People tend to cycle on and off Medicaid for various reasons, but the Congressional Budget Office projects the average monthly enrollment for 2016 will be 77 million Americans, and the total number who will enroll at some point during the year will be 98 million.

Medicaid's Perverse Incentives

The federal government's method for distributing Medicaid funds to states encourages fraud, creates perverse incentives for state officials, and encourages states to expand their programs to people who don't need assistance. Because federal and state governments share the burden of Medicaid spending, neither side cares about the drawbacks of the program—induced dependence, waste, and fraud—as much as they should.

The more a state spends on its Medicaid program, the more it receives from the federal government. When a state spends $1, it receives between $1 and $3 from the federal government. States can thus double, triple, or even quadruple their money by spending more on Medicaid. This leads state and federal officials to tolerate stunning amounts of fraud. The Government Accountability Office consistently designates Medicaid as a "high-risk" program: official estimates of improper Medicaid payments suggest the federal share alone was $17.5 billion in 2014.

The system of matching federal funds creates perverse incentives for state officials to spend too much on Medicaid and too little on other priorities. Spending $1 on police buys $1 of police protection. Spending $1 on Medicaid, however, buys $2 to $4 of medical or long-term care. States tend to spend the marginal dollar on Medicaid even when spending it on police, education, or transportation would provide greater benefits.

The perverse incentives are even greater under the ACA's Medicaid expansion. States that want to reduce state spending by $1 million would have to cut outlays in the "old" Medicaid program by anywhere from $2 million to $5 million. (The additional savings revert to the federal government.) By contrast, since states pay only 10 percent of the cost of the Medicaid expansion, states must cut Medicaid-expansion outlays by

$10 million in order to achieve $1 million of budgetary savings. In other words, the Medicaid expansion creates perverse incentives for states to cut health care spending on needier individuals rather than less-needy individuals. Cutting health care for able-bodied adults requires state officials to inflict up to five times more political pain than cutting health care for needier, more-vulnerable enrollees.

Medicaid both pulls and pushes enrollees into dependence. Medicaid makes private health care less affordable—thus pushing people into the program. Economists Mark Duggan and Fiona Scott Morton found that Medicaid's system of setting drug prices increases prices for private payers by 13 percent. The more federal and state governments expand Medicaid, the more expensive private medical care and insurance become.

Medicaid, historically, has paid health care providers directly, on a fee-for-service basis. However, states often contract with private insurers to provide Medicaid benefits to enrollees in the hope of making the program more efficient. Currently some 60 percent of enrollees receive Medicaid benefits through private insurers. This practice creates some of the same problems as in Medicare (see Chapter 6). Once states determine how much they will pay insurers per enrollee, insurers identify and recruit Medicaid-eligible individuals who will cost them less than that amount—pulling them into the system. These are often healthy people who were eligible for Medicaid but never enrolled. Whatever unnecessary expenditures these "private" Medicaid plans might avoid, the added costs of new enrollees swamp those savings. One study found that when California decided to "switch from fee-for-service to managed care," there was "a substantial increase in government spending but no corresponding improvement in infant health outcomes. The findings cast doubt on the hypothesis that health maintenance organization (HMO) contracting has reduced the strain on government budgets." Overall, contracting with private carriers tends not to reduce Medicaid spending in the average state.

The State Children's Health Insurance Program

Congress created the State Children's Health Insurance Program in 1997 to expand health insurance coverage among children in families that earn too much to be eligible for Medicaid. The federal government funds each state's program much as it funds traditional Medicaid, but with two main differences. First, states receive a larger federal match under SCHIP than under traditional Medicaid. In 2017, the federal government will pay for at least 88 percent of the cost of each state's program because the

ACA authorized a temporary increase in the federal share. For every dollar that states invest in SCHIP, they can "pull down" at least $7 from the federal government (i.e., from taxpayers in other states).

Second, the federal government ostensibly limits the amount it will contribute to each state's program. But the cap is not as binding as it appears. States often burn through their federal SCHIP funds before the end of the fiscal year and then demand additional funds. In effect, states create an emergency situation, daring Congress to throw sick children off the SCHIP rolls. Congress has repeatedly bailed out such states, effectively rewarding them for committing to spend more federal dollars than federal law allows.

As a result of these perverse incentives, states have expanded SCHIP eligibility dramatically. Nineteen states offer SCHIP to families of four with incomes of $73,000 or more. In New York, SCHIP is available to families of four earning $98,000 annually. Because SCHIP targets families higher up the income scale than Medicaid does, and because higher-income families are more likely to have health insurance to begin with, SCHIP leads to even greater "crowd-out" of private insurance than Medicaid.

Are Medicaid and SCHIP Even Helping?

Remarkably, there is little reliable evidence that these programs have a net positive effect on health, and absolutely no evidence they are the best way to improve the health of targeted populations.

Critics argue that despite the expense, Medicaid is lousy coverage. The Government Accountability Office reports that, compared with privately insured individuals, Medicaid enrollees notoriously have "greater difficulty accessing specialty and dental care," and "over two-thirds of children in Medicaid with a potential mental health need did not receive mental health services."

A study by John Bates Clark Medal-winning economist Amy Finkelstein and other top health economists examined the effects of Oregon's decision to expand Medicaid in 2008. The Oregon Health Insurance Experiment randomly assigned applicants to receive Medicaid or nothing, and then compared outcomes for the two groups. As it happens, the study's participants were drawn from the same vulnerable population targeted by the ACA's Medicaid expansion. Random assignment made this experiment the most reliable study ever conducted on the effects of health insurance. The authors found that "Medicaid coverage generated no significant improvements in measured physical health outcomes in the first 2 years, but it did increase use of health care services, raise rates of diabetes detection and management, lower rates of depression, and reduce financial strain."

The authors chose measures of physical health that should have been amenable to treatment over a two-year period. Yet Medicaid produced no improvement in the people it served compared with the people who got no coverage. Like Finkelstein's study that found no effect of Medicare on elderly mortality in that program's first decade (see Chapter 6), the lack of any improvement in physical health outcomes among Medicaid enrollees should throw a stop sign in front of Medicaid generally and the ACA's Medicaid expansion in particular.

Similarly, there is no evidence that Medicaid is cost effective. The Oregon Health Insurance Experiment did find small improvements in self-reported mental health. But not even that study attempted to quantify whether Medicaid is a cost-effective way of achieving those gains—that is, whether state and federal governments could have purchased better health by spending those funds differently.

Whether or not Medicaid, SCHIP, or the ACA's premium subsidies turn out to improve health for some populations, or to be a cost-effective way of doing so, these programs become increasingly less cost effective the higher up the income scale they reach. Higher-income households have higher baseline access to health insurance and medical care. As these programs move up the income scale, they offer taxpayer-financed coverage to increasing numbers of people who already had private insurance. The 82 percent crowd-out estimate mentioned previously suggests the ACA's Medicaid expansion could be covering fewer than 2 previously uninsured Americans for the price of 10.

Federal and state governments should not continue to take trillions of dollars from taxpayers to support these programs when they don't even know what they are buying.

Investigate Whether Medicaid Is Actually Helping

Rather than expand Medicaid, federal and state policymakers should conduct further experiments to determine what benefits Medicaid and SCHIP actually produce and whether other uses of those funds would produce greater gains in health and financial security. Policymakers should model these studies on the Oregon Health Insurance Experiment. The studies should be conducted with existing populations rather than new enrollees, so as not to impose additional burdens on taxpayers.

States should apply for waivers from the federal government to conduct such studies. Where federal law does not provide authority for the Secretary of Health and Human Services to approve such waivers, Congress should create such authority or enact legislation directly approving such studies.

Critics will object to randomly assigning some Medicaid enrollees to receive no coverage. Such criticism makes the mistake of assuming that Medicaid improves health when that is exactly what we do not know and precisely why states need to conduct such studies. It is unethical to preserve or expand Medicaid without knowing whether it even helps its presumed beneficiaries. The ethical course is to determine whether Medicaid is cost effective. That requires random assignment.

Refuse the ACA's Medicaid Expansion

States that have implemented the Medicaid expansion are buckling under the expense. The program is costing states far more than they or the federal government projected. In 2015, the cost was $6,366 per enrollee, nearly 50 percent more than the federal government projected. The cost to states will be even higher because enrollment in implementing states has exceeded projections by an average 91 percent. Enrollment has even exceeded *maximum*-enrollment projections by an average 73 percent.

The 19 states that dodged those bullets by refusing to implement the Medicaid expansion should continue to refuse. The 31 states that have implemented it should withdraw from the program.

Repeal the ACA

Without reliable evidence of cost-effectiveness, neither those 31 states nor Congress can justify the Medicaid expansion, particularly when every penny Congress spends on it adds to the federal debt. Congress should repeal the ACA's Medicaid expansion along with the rest of that act. Repealing the Medicaid expansion alone would reduce federal spending and deficits by $969 billion from 2017 through 2026 and eliminate the low-wage trap that the program creates. Repealing the remainder of the ACA would eliminate the low-wage traps its exchange subsidies create, while reducing the cost of private health insurance for the vast majority of enrollees of those programs.

The ACA remains an unpopular law. Nineteen states have rejected its Medicaid expansion. Those states have reduced federal spending, federal deficits, and the future tax burden of taxpayers in *all* states. Projections by the Urban Institute indicate that those 19 states will save taxpayers $349 billion by 2022. It is unfair to force taxpayers in states that have rejected the Medicaid expansion to pay for the expansion in the other states.

Reform Medicaid and SCHIP

Repealing the ACA is not enough, however. It makes little sense for taxpayers to send money to Washington, only for Congress to send those funds back to their state capitols with strings and perverse incentives attached. Congress should devolve control over Medicaid and SCHIP to the states.

In 1996, Congress eliminated the federal entitlement to a welfare check, placed a five-year limit on cash assistance, and froze federal spending on such assistance. It then distributed those funds to the states in the form of block grants with fewer federal restrictions. The results were unquestionably positive. Welfare rolls were cut in half, and poverty reached the lowest point in a generation.

The federal government should emulate that success by eliminating all federal entitlements to Medicaid and SCHIP benefits, freezing federal Medicaid and SCHIP spending at current levels, and distributing those funds to the states as unrestricted block grants. Congressional Budget Office projections indicate that simply freezing federal Medicaid and SCHIP spending at 2016 levels would produce $945 billion in savings and deficit reduction by 2026. Together with repeal of the ACA's Medicaid expansion, block grants would reduce projected federal deficits from 2017 through 2026 by roughly 20 percent.

With full flexibility and full responsibility for the marginal Medicaid dollar, states could then decide whether and how to navigate the Samaritan's dilemma. States that want to focus only on their neediest residents could do so and put the savings toward other priorities like police or tax reduction. States that want to spend more on their Medicaid programs would be free to raise taxes to do so, and vice versa, without federal strictures. States would learn from the successes and failures of each other's experiments. Since states would bear the full marginal cost of their reformed Medicaid programs or successor programs, they would be more likely to conduct randomized, controlled experiments to determine the most cost-effective uses of those funds.

As an alternative to the current system of matching grants, some members of Congress have proposed that the federal government contribute to each state's Medicaid program through "per capita block grants." In that case, the federal government would provide states with a fixed amount of funds per Medicaid enrollee. Per capita block grants would eliminate the incentive that the current matching-grant system creates for states to offer more benefits to enrollees. Indeed, they could encourage states to offer less coverage and even worse access to providers. Unfortunately, this proposal would not encourage states to remove from their Medicaid rolls people who could obtain coverage on their own. On the contrary, it would preserve the current incentive for states to add more and more nonneedy people to their Medicaid rolls.

Block grants like those used in welfare reform would eliminate the perverse incentives that induce dependence, favor Medicaid and SCHIP spending over other priorities, lead states to tolerate widespread fraud, and encourage states themselves to defraud federal taxpayers. Over time, the federal government should give the states full responsibility for Medicaid by eliminating federal Medicaid spending while concomitantly cutting federal taxes. States can hasten these reforms by pressuring the federal government for maximum flexibility in administering their Medicaid programs.

Suggested Readings

Antonisse, Larisa, Rachel Garfield, Robin Rudowitz, and Samantha Artiga. "The Effects of Medicaid Expansion under the ACA: Findings from a Literature Review." Kaiser Commission on Medicaid and the Uninsured Issue Brief, June 2016.

Bitler, Marianne P., and Madeline Zavodny. "Medicaid: A Review of the Literature." National Bureau of Economic Research Working Paper no. w20169, May 2014.

Borjas, George J. "Welfare Reform, Labor Supply, and Health Insurance in the Immigrant Population." *Journal of Health Economics* 22, no. 6 (November 2003): 933–58.

Cannon, Michael F. "Entitlement Bandits." *National Review*, July 4, 2011.

———. "Medicaid's Unseen Costs." Cato Institute Policy Analysis no. 548, August 18, 2005.

———. "Should Ohio Expand Medicaid?" Testimony before the Subcommittee on Health and Human Services, Finance and Appropriations Committee, Ohio House of Representatives, March 13, 2013.

———. "Sinking SCHIP: A First Step toward Stopping the Growth of Government Health Programs." Cato Institute Briefing Paper no. 99, September 13, 2007.

Cannon, Michael F., and Michael D. Tanner. *Healthy Competition: What's Holding Back Health Care and How to Free It.* Washington: Cato Institute, 2007.

Duggan, Mark, and Tamara Hayford. "Has the Shift to Managed Care Reduced Medicaid Expenditures? Evidence from State and Local-Level Mandates." *Journal of Policy Analysis and Management* 32, no. 3 (2013).

La Couture, Brittany. "Termination of Medicaid for Inmates." American Action Forum Insight, July 7, 2016.

Moses, Stephen. "Aging America's Achilles' Heel: Medicaid Long-Term Care." Cato Institute Policy Analysis no. 549, September 1, 2005.

—Prepared by Michael F. Cannon

6. Medicare

Medicare is a $600 billion federal entitlement program that provides health insurance to nearly 60 million Americans who are elderly or disabled or meet other criteria. It is the largest purchaser of health care goods and services in the world and effectively controls even more of the U.S. health care sector than federal Medicare outlays suggest. It is also the single greatest obstacle to making U.S. health care better, more affordable, and more secure.

Medicare is lousy health insurance. When people complain about excessive U.S. health spending, they are complaining about Medicare. When they complain about the fee-for-service payment system; about wasteful care, harmful care, and medical errors; about health care fraud and excessive profits; about federal deficits and debt, the time bomb of entitlement spending, and special-interest influence over health care; about the lack of innovation, evidence-based medicine, electronic medical records, accountable care organizations, telemedicine, and coordinated care, they are complaining in every case about *Medicare.*

Since 1965, Medicare has blocked innovations that would improve health care, to say nothing of how it has denied workers the right to control their earnings. Supporters claim that Medicare is more efficient than private insurance because it has lower administrative costs. To reach that conclusion, they ignore many of Medicare's administrative costs, in particular the "excess burden" of taxation, or the reduction in economic output caused by all the taxes necessary to finance Medicare spending. Estimates place those costs between 20 percent and 100 percent of Medicare expenditures, dwarfing any administrative costs of private insurance. Decades of reports by government watchdogs demonstrate that the main way Medicare avoids administrative costs is by failing to conduct oversight. The result is rampant waste and fraud. The Government Accountability Office reports that 13 percent of traditional Medicare payments in 2014 were fraudulent or improper. Medicare's low administrative spending is one of its flaws, not one of its virtues.

Perhaps Medicare's only success has been to concentrate power in Washington, D.C. It is indeed popular among enrollees—not because it is better than the alternatives, but because it has eliminated better alternatives and thereby made seniors and the disabled utterly dependent on the government for their health care.

Low-Quality Care

A landmark study by economists Amy Finkelstein and Robin McKnight made the following conclusion:

> Using several different empirical approaches, we find no evidence that the introduction of nearly universal health insurance for the elderly had an impact on overall elderly mortality in its first 10 years. . . . Our findings suggest that Medicare did not play a role in the substantial declines in elderly mortality that immediately followed the introduction of Medicare.

The authors estimated that the reduction in out-of-pocket medical spending among seniors that followed Medicare's introduction produced benefits of less than 40 percent of the program's total cost. Data limitations prevented them from estimating any nonmortality health benefits from Medicare. Nevertheless, at a minimum, Medicare appears not to have saved a single life in its first decade, calling into question whether the program has been net beneficial. Elsewhere, Finkelstein found evidence that Medicare has been a driving force behind the growth of health spending on both the elderly and the nonelderly.

Additional evidence suggests Medicare may not pass a cost–benefit test. The Dartmouth Atlas of Health Care and other researchers estimate that a third or more of Medicare spending provides no value whatsoever: it makes the patient no healthier or happier. If we were to add to that figure spending on services whose costs exceed the benefit to the patient, it would show an even larger share of Medicare spending to be wasteful. Medicare may be one of the factors behind the United States' leading role in developing new diagnostic tests and medical treatments. If so, it appears that once those goods and services become available, Medicare pays for them whether or not they benefit a particular patient.

One factor that contributes to the epidemic of wasteful Medicare spending is that the program generally provides open-ended subsidies for whatever medical care providers recommend. The Medicare Payment Advisory Commission (MedPAC) is a federal bureaucracy that advises Congress on how to set prices and other terms of exchange with Medicare-participating providers. MedPAC itself reported the following:

> Medicare, the largest single payer in the system, pays all of its health care providers without differentiation based on quality. Providers who improve quality are not rewarded for their efforts. In fact, Medicare often pays *more* when a serious illness or injury occurs or recurs while patients are under the system's care. The incentives of this system are neutral or negative toward improving the quality of care. [emphasis added]

Medicare generally pays providers on a "fee-for-service" basis, meaning a separate fee for each individual service or hospitalization, rather than paying for a particular health outcome (which can be exceedingly difficult) or paying a fixed or "capitated" amount per patient. Fee-for-service payment has benefits: it gives patients a wide choice of providers, for example. However, it creates incentives for providers to recommend services that offer little or no benefit, even services that end up being harmful. It allows multiple providers to treat a shared patient without coordinating their efforts (a job that then falls to the patient). Medicare even rewards medical errors and punishes efforts to reduce them. When a medical error results in the patient's requiring more services, Medicare pays for the initial, harmful service and pays *again* for the remedial care. Medicare thus pays hospitals and other providers less when they improve the quality of care by reducing medical errors. This system fuels the problems of wasteful spending and medical errors.

By heavily subsidizing fee-for-service payments and fragmented delivery, Medicare prevents competition that could lead to alternative ways of financing and delivering medical care. A market system would find ways to reduce wasteful care and medical errors and to promote coordinated care, electronic medical records, effectiveness research, and evidence-based medicine. In particular, Medicare has inhibited competition from integrated, prepaid group plans such as Kaiser Permanente and Group Health Cooperative. Along with other government interventions—such as clinician licensing and the tax preference for employer-sponsored insurance—Medicare has dramatically tilted the playing field in favor of fee-for-service payment and uncoordinated care.

Congress has attempted to mitigate the perverse incentives and unintended consequences of Medicare's payment systems. Various tweaks and demonstration programs have tried to eliminate financial rewards for medical errors, promote coordinated care, and fund effectiveness research.

Yet demonstration programs aimed at improving quality or reducing spending in Medicare have not been successful.

The Dinosaur's Veto

There are *reasons* such efforts are not successful. Any effort to increase quality or reduce costs in Medicare represents a threat to high-cost, low-quality providers. If those efforts are voluntary, inefficient providers just avoid them and keep getting paid for doing what they have always done. Analyst Robert Laszewski describes this dynamic in the context of the Affordable Care Act's (ACA) attempt to promote "accountable care organizations" (ACOs). "Here's a flash for the policy wonks pushing ACOs: They only work if the provider gets paid less for the same patient population. Why would they be dumb enough to voluntarily accept that outcome?"

Reforms intended to force Medicare-participating providers to become more efficient usually die under intense lobbying from the high-cost, low-quality providers who stand to lose. A market system would force those providers out of business. Instead, Medicare creates a dinosaur's veto that allows lousy providers to protect their revenue streams and sticks Medicare patients and taxpayers with low-quality, high-cost care.

Medicare Advantage

One bright spot, of sorts, is the Medicare Advantage program. Traditionally, Medicare has been a government-run health insurance scheme that writes checks directly to doctors, hospitals, and other providers. In the Medicare Advantage program, the government pays insurance companies to play that role. Medicare enrollees may choose among competing Medicare Advantage plans, which often offer more coverage than traditional Medicare. Some 30 percent of enrollees opt for Medicare Advantage plans, a share the Congressional Budget Office projects will grow to 40 percent by 2026. In effect, Medicare Advantage plans compete for enrollees against the "public option" of traditional Medicare.

Medicare Advantage creates more competition in the delivery of medicine by extending government subsidies to different ways of financing and organizing health care. Some Medicare Advantage plans are fully integrated and capitated plans, such as Kaiser Permanente. Others are fee-for-service plans like traditional Medicare. Other plans fall somewhere in between.

Medicare Advantage mitigates some of the problems traditional Medicare creates. A former chief executive of Kaiser Permanente—the original accountable care organization—noted that the ACA's effort to tweak traditional Medicare's payment systems "is not as good as [the] Medicare Advantage program" at promoting integrated, accountable care. One review of the literature found that Medicare Advantage plans score higher on some quality measures, including use of preventive care. Medicare Advantage health maintenance organizations appear to do a better job of avoiding unnecessary hospitalizations and encouraging less-expensive care. One study estimated that Medicare Advantage plans reduce hospitalizations by a third without any negative impact on mortality. Medicare Advantage appears to have spillover effects that reduce unnecessary spending in traditional Medicare.

There is nothing inherently superior about the government writing checks to insurance companies instead of health care providers, however. There is evidence Medicare pays more to cover enrollees through Medicare Advantage than it would cost to cover them through traditional Medicare. The projected growth in Medicare Advantage enrollment suggests this may be the case. This may be because participating insurers tend to market themselves to Medicare enrollees who will cost them less (and to avoid patients who would cost them more) than the government is paying. The result is akin to the dynamic in the ACA's Exchanges: government-determined prices lead insurers to make their plans attractive to relatively healthy enrollees and unattractive to relatively sick enrollees. Traditional Medicare receives higher marks from enrollees with expensive illnesses, likely because it provides relatively—albeit dangerously—easy access to care.

To build on the meager progress of Medicare Advantage, Congress should take three steps to liberalize health care for the elderly and disabled.

Reform: Sever the Tie between Medicare and Social Security

At present, people who are eligible for Medicare but do not enroll forfeit all Social Security benefits—past and future. Conditions on government subsidies become problematic when they require recipients to accept a second government subsidy. The main problem with this condition, however, is that it has no basis in statute. Federal bureaucrats just made it up. It is fairly clear why they did. Withholding Social Security benefits makes it harder for seniors to leave Medicare, which has the effect of both quashing the market for alternative forms of health insurance and making more Americans dependent on Medicare.

Congress should allow seniors to opt out of Medicare without losing Social Security benefits. Removing this condition would curb executive overreach, expand the market for alternatives to Medicare, and create a political constituency of seniors that is more open to fundamental Medicare reform.

Reform: Make Medicare like Social Security

The single, most dramatic thing Congress can do to make health care better, more affordable, and more secure is to take the $600 billion it currently spends on Medicare and simply give it to Medicare enrollees as cash. Currently, Medicare sends those billions to providers and insurers, who fight fiercely to protect their revenue streams, and who can increase their haul by providing more low-quality services or lobbying for greater subsidies. Seniors often join providers and insurers to lobby for protecting or expanding access to low-quality care—because it is taxpayers' money on the line, not their own. The rules Medicare attaches to these subsidies stifle innovation, while keeping quality low and costs high.

One bipartisan proposal would create a more level playing field between traditional Medicare and private plans. "Premium support" would give enrollees a fixed subsidy they could apply toward either traditional Medicare or the private health plan of their choice. A fixed subsidy would encourage enrollees to choose less wasteful coverage. If enrollees chose plans that cost more than their premium subsidy, they would pay the balance. If they chose a less expensive plan, they could keep the unspent portion of their subsidy, perhaps in a health savings account. A level playing field would reveal to enrollees the full cost of all health plans and allow enrollees to decide which ones provide the greatest value. Efficient and innovative health plans would thrive. The rest would not.

Premium support is a step in the right direction. It would acclimate more enrollees to choosing their health plans and being cost-conscious consumers. But Medicare would continue to suppress desperately needed innovations. And the government would still be in the business of specifying rules for participating insurers (e.g., what types of coverage they must offer) and prices and other terms of exchange for providers participating in traditional Medicare. It is simply not possible to level the playing field between government and private-sector competitors. For example, private insurers pay taxes; government programs don't.

Converting Medicare into a program like Social Security—that is, distributing cash to beneficiaries—would spark an innovation revolution.

Enrollees could receive "Medicare checks" at the same time they receive their Social Security checks. Medicare checks would average more than $10,000 per enrollee per year. Enrollees could use those funds to purchase the health plan of their choice at actuarially fair rates. Enrollees who want more expensive health insurance could supplement their subsidy with private funds, just as they do now with Medicare Advantage and Medigap plans. Alternatively, seniors who choose a lower-cost plan could save their extra health care dollars in a tax-free health savings account.

The size of each enrollee's Medicare check would depend on their health status and income. When an individual enrolls in the program, Medicare would use competitive bidding or risk-adjustment formulas to adjust the amount of that enrollee's check according to that individual enrollee's health status. It would use Social Security Administration data to calibrate the amount of the enrollee's check according to the enrollee's lifetime income. Low-income and sicker enrollees would get Medicare checks large enough to enable them to afford a standard package of insurance benefits. Healthier and higher-income enrollees would get smaller checks. As with Social Security, enrollees would then be free to spend that money as they see fit. They could use their Medicare checks to purchase whatever health plan they choose, to purchase preexisting conditions insurance, to save for future medical expenses, or to purchase other items, like tuition for their grandchildren. The availability of guaranteed-renewable health insurance, and the fact that Medicare would use lifetime rather than current income to adjust for income, means Medicare would only need to adjust for income and health status once, at enrollment. If enrollment growth times medical inflation grows faster than gross domestic product (GDP), Medicare would reduce checks for healthier and higher-income enrollees to preserve the ability of sicker and low-income enrollees to afford a standard package of insurance benefits.

Critics worry that, to the extent the risk-adjustment does not perfectly track the risk of health claims, some enrollees would have insufficient funds to purchase health plans at actuarially fair rates. This objection fails for two reasons. First, to the extent Medicare's competitive-bidding processes or risk-adjustment formulas are imperfect, they are already harming the sick by leading Medicare Advantage plans to avoid relatively sick enrollees. Second, even when the government imperfectly calibrates the amount, giving the money to enrollees would create incentives for insurers to find innovative ways to cover the sick, rather than to avoid them. If Medicare can risk-adjust the payments it makes to insurance companies, then there is no reason not to give that money directly to enrollees.

Another objection is that, whereas Medicare currently offers an open-ended entitlement to health care subsidies, giving enrollees a fixed subsidy means some enrollees would run out of money. That could happen if enrollees' current income and assets were less than their lifetime income would suggest, or if enrollees frittered away their subsidy. Implicit in the latter concern is the worry that Medicare enrollees could not spend $600 billion as competently as government bureaucrats can. This objection likewise fails. If any enrollees were to run out of money, they would most likely become eligible for Medicaid (see Chapter 5).

More important, enrollees are unlikely to run out of money because consumers can make $600 billion go a lot farther than the government can. First, subsidizing seniors with cash would encourage cost-saving innovations. Medicare enrollees would spend that $600 billion much more cost-consciously when it is *their* money than when it is the taxpayers' money. That would put downward pressure on prices in a way Medicare simply cannot. Enrollee cost-consciousness would spark and reward innovations like the "reverse deductibles" that have led to price reductions of thousands or tens of thousands of dollars. Second, it would remove regulatory barriers to such innovations. Removing Medicare from its role as a purchaser of medical services would eliminate the restrictive price and exchange controls that have stifled innovation in health care delivery. Finally, Medicare checks would come with a built-in buffer. Ironically, the fact that Medicare likely wastes at least one out of every three dollars means enrollees could waste one-third or more of that $600 billion without any adverse health effects for the average enrollee. All that wasteful Medicare spending is usually a problem. When reforming Medicare, it is an absolute boon.

Reforming Medicare by letting enrollees control that $600 billion would end federal micromanagement of the health care sector. It would spark an innovation revolution by allowing the consumers' choices and competition—rather than a government bureaucracy—to determine prices, payment systems, delivery systems, and how to reward quality. It would unlock the potential of integrated delivery systems, effectiveness research, coordinated care, and other reforms that Medicare is struggling—and failing—to deliver. Just as Medicare has spillover effects that increase costs for non-Medicare patients, and just as Medicare Advantage has spillover effects that reduce spending in traditional Medicare, both elderly and nonelderly patients would see the benefits of these innovations in the form of better, more affordable, and more secure health care.

Reform: Prefund Retiree Health Care

Finally, Congress should replace Medicare's inequitable system of intergenerational transfers with a prefunded system in which workers invest their Medicare taxes in personal accounts dedicated to their own health needs in retirement. Congress should allow workers to put their full Medicare payroll tax payment in a personal savings account. Workers could invest those funds in a number of vehicles and augment those funds in retirement with other savings. Over time, Congress could make contributions to these personal accounts voluntary.

This proposal for Medicare personal accounts is similar to many Social Security reform proposals (see Chapter 7). One similarity is that diverting workers' tax payments into personal accounts would make it difficult to pay current benefits. Congress could make up much of those "transition costs" by cutting Medicare outlays. As noted earlier, an estimated one-third of Medicare outlays do nothing to improve beneficiaries' health or make them any happier. Thus, Congress could allow per-enrollee Medicare spending to grow at a rate less than GDP without harming the health of enrollees. If Congress is unable or unwilling to cover all transition costs by reducing Medicare outlays, it should make up the gap by cutting other government spending (see Chapter 1)—not by raising taxes.

Suggested Readings

Cannon, Michael F. "Entitlement Bandits." *National Review*, July 4, 2011.
———. "Fannie Med? Why a 'Public Option' Is Hazardous to Your Health." Cato Institute Policy Analysis no. 642, August 6, 2009.
Cannon, Michael F., and Alain Enthoven. "Markets Beat Government on Medical Errors." *American Spectator*, May 13, 2008.
Cannon, Michael F., and Michael D. Tanner. *Healthy Competition: What's Holding Back Health Care and How to Free It*. Washington: Cato Institute, 2007.
Christianson, Jon B., and George Avery. "Prepaid Group Practice and Health Care Policy." In *Toward a 21st Century Health System: The Contributions and Promise of Prepaid Group Practice*, edited by Alain C. Enthoven and Laura A. Tollen. San Francisco, CA: Jossey-Bass, 2004.
Cohen, Diane, and Michael F. Cannon. "The Independent Payment Advisory Board: PPACA's Anti-Constitutional and Authoritarian Super-Legislature." Cato Institute Policy Analysis no. 700, June 14, 2012.
Edwards, Chris, and Michael F. Cannon. "Medicare Reforms." Cato Institute. DownsizingGovernment.org, September 1, 2010.
Hyman, David A. *Medicare Meets Mephistopheles*. Washington: Cato Institute, 2006.
Kling, Arnold. *Crisis of Abundance: Rethinking How We Pay for Health Care*. Washington: Cato Institute, 2006.
Pauly, Mark V. *Markets without Magic: How Competition Might Save Medicare*. Washington: American Enterprise Institute, 2008.

Saving, Thomas S., and Andrew Rettenmaier. *The Diagnosis and Treatment of Medicare.* Washington: American Enterprise Institute, 2007.

U.S. Congressional Budget Office. "Lessons from Medicare's Demonstration Projects on Disease Management, Care Coordination, and Value-Based Payment." Issue Brief, January 2012.

—Prepared by Michael F. Cannon

7. Social Security

Although Congress and the Trump administration don't want to discuss it, the Social Security system faces severe financial pressures. Social Security's long-term unfunded liabilities now total $32.1 trillion. Congress's failure to act is threatening America's economic stability and promises to bury our children and grandchildren under a mountain of debt. Reform is not an option, it is a necessity, and Congress should act now.

But all Social Security reforms are not equal. Raising taxes and cutting benefits would have their own economic costs and would make a bad deal even worse for today's younger workers. However, by allowing younger workers to privately invest their Social Security taxes through individual accounts, we can

- help restore Social Security to long-term solvency, without massive tax increases;
- provide workers with higher benefits than Social Security would otherwise be able to pay;
- create a system that treats women, minorities, and young people more fairly;
- increase national savings and economic growth;
- allow low-income workers to accumulate real, inheritable wealth for the first time in their lives; and
- give workers ownership and control over their retirement funds.

The Looming Crisis

Social Security is a "pay-as-you-go" (PAYGO) program, in which Social Security taxes are used to immediately pay benefits for current retirees. It is not a "funded plan," in which contributions are collected and invested in financial assets and then liquidated and converted into a pension at retirement. Rather, it is a simple wealth transfer from current workers to current retirees.

Table 7.1
PAYGO Social Security System

Generation	Period 1	Period 2	Period 3	Period 4
0	Retired **benefits**	Dead	Dead	Dead
1	↑ Working ↑ **contributions**	Retired **benefits**	Dead	Dead
2	Unborn	↑ Working ↑ **contributions**	Retired **benefits**	Dead
3	Unborn	Unborn	↑ Working ↑ **contributions**	Retired **benefits**
4	Unborn	Unborn	Unborn	↑ Working ↑ **contributions**

SOURCE: Thomas Siems, "Reengineering Social Security for the New Economy," Cato Institute Social Security Paper no. 22, January 23, 2001.

Table 7.1 shows a basic model of overlapping generations: people are born in every time period, live for two periods (the first as workers, the second as retirees), and finally die. As time passes, older generations are replaced by younger generations. The columns represent successive time periods, and the rows represent successive generations. Each generation is labeled by the period of its birth, so that Generation 1 is born in Period 1, and so on. In each period, two generations overlap, with younger workers coexisting with older retirees.

In Table 7.1, a PAYGO pension system provides a start-up bonus to Generation 0 retirees by taking contributions from Generation 1 workers to pay benefits to those already retired. Thus, Generation 0 retirees receive a windfall because they never paid taxes into the system. Subsequent generations both pay taxes and receive benefits. There is no direct relationship between taxes paid and benefits received.

As long as the wage base supporting Social Security grows faster than the number of recipients, the program can continue to pay higher benefits to those recipients. But the growth in the labor force has slowed dramatically. In 1950, for example, there were 16.5 covered workers for every retiree receiving benefits from the program. Since then, Americans have been living longer and having fewer babies. As a result, there are now just 2.8 covered workers per beneficiary; and by 2034, there will be only 2.2

Figure 7.1
Worker to Beneficiary Ratio, 1945–2090

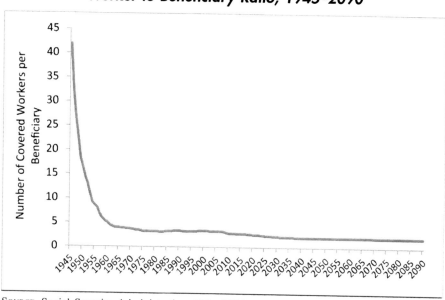

SOURCE: Social Security Administration, "The 2016 Annual Report of the Board of Trustees of the Federal Old-Age and Survivors Insurance and Federal Disability Insurance Trust Funds," Table IV.B3, Covered Workers and Beneficiaries, Calendar Years 1945–2090. Washington: Government Printing Office, 2016.

(Figure 7.1). Real wage growth (especially in wages below the payroll tax cap) has not been nearly fast enough to offset this demographic shift.

As Figure 7.2 shows, Social Security is already running a cash-flow deficit. In 2016, for instance, the program will pay out roughly $70 billion more in benefits than it takes in through taxes. That might seem a small amount of money in a world of trillion-dollar deficits, but without reform this shortfall will continue to grow. Very soon Social Security's deficit will reach levels that threaten to explode our overall budget deficit. Along with Medicare and Medicaid, Social Security will be one of the major drivers of our country's long-term debt.

In theory, of course, Social Security is supposed to continue paying benefits by drawing on the Social Security Trust Fund until 2034, after which the Trust Fund will be exhausted. At that point, *by law,* Social Security benefits will have to be cut by approximately 21 percent.

In reality, the Social Security Trust Fund is not an asset that can be used to pay benefits. Perhaps the best description of the Trust Fund can be found in the Clinton administration's fiscal year 2000 budget:

Figure 7.2
Cash Flow Deficit, 2015–2025

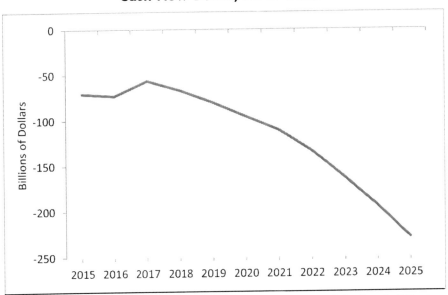

SOURCE: Social Security Administration, "The 2016 Annual Report of the Board of Trustees of the Federal Old-Age and Survivors Insurance and Federal Disability Insurance Trust Funds," Table IV.A3, Operations of the Combined OASI and DI Trust Funds, Calendar Years 2011–2025. Washington: Government Printing Office, 2016.

NOTE: OASI = Old-Age and Survivors Insurance; DI = Disability Insurance. Intermediate scenario for years 2016–2025: payroll tax contributions and taxation of benefits are included, while net interest income is not.

These [Trust Fund] balances are available to finance future benefit payments and other Trust Fund expenditures—but only in a bookkeeping sense. . . . They do not consist of real economic assets that can be drawn down in the future to fund benefits. Instead, they are claims on the Treasury that, when redeemed, will have to be financed by raising taxes, borrowing from the public, or reducing benefits or other expenditures. The existence of large Trust Fund balances, therefore, does not, by itself, have any impact on the Government's ability to pay benefits.

Even if Congress can find a way to redeem the bonds, the Trust Fund surplus will be completely exhausted by 2034. At that point, Social Security will have to rely solely on revenue from the payroll tax—but that revenue will not be sufficient to pay all promised benefits. Overall, Social Security faces unfunded liabilities of $32.1 trillion over the infinite horizon. Clearly, Social Security is not sustainable in its current form. That means that

Congress will again be forced to resort to raising taxes and/or cutting benefits to enable the program to stumble along.

In fact, the Social Security statement mailed to workers contains this caveat:

> Your estimated benefits are based on current law. Congress has made changes to the law in the past and can do so at any time. The law governing benefit amounts may change because, by 2034, the payroll taxes collected will be enough to pay only about 79 percent of scheduled benefits.

Other Issues with Social Security

Social Security taxes are already so high, relative to benefits, that Social Security has quite simply become a bad deal for younger workers, providing a poor, below-market rate of return. This poor rate of return means that many young workers' retirement benefits will be far lower than if they were able to invest those funds privately.

In addition, Social Security taxes displace private savings options, resulting in a large net loss of national savings, reducing capital investment, wages, national income, and economic growth. Moreover, by increasing the cost of hiring workers, the payroll tax substantially reduces wages, employment, and economic growth as well.

After all the economic analysis, however, perhaps the single most important reason for transforming Social Security into a system of individual accounts is that it would give American workers true ownership of and control over their retirement benefits.

Many Americans believe that Social Security is an "earned right." That is, because they have paid Social Security taxes, they are entitled to receive Social Security benefits. The government encourages this belief by referring to Social Security taxes as "contributions," as in the Federal Insurance Contributions Act (FICA). However, in the case of *Flemming v. Nestor*, the U.S. Supreme Court ruled that workers have no legally binding contractual or property right to their Social Security benefits and those benefits can be changed, cut, or even taken away at any time.

As the Court stated, "To engraft upon Social Security a concept of 'accrued property rights' would deprive it of the flexibility and boldness in adjustment to ever changing conditions which it demands." That decision built on a previous case, *Helvering v. Davis*, in which the Court had ruled that Social Security is not a contributory insurance program, stating that "the proceeds of both the employer and employee taxes are to be paid into the Treasury like any other internal revenue generally, and are not earmarked in any way."

In effect, Social Security turns older Americans into supplicants, dependent on the political process for their retirement benefits. If they work hard, play by the rules, and pay Social Security taxes their entire lives, they earn the privilege of going hat in hand to the government and hoping that politicians decide to give them some money for retirement.

Options for Reform

There are few options for dealing with the problem. This is not an opinion shared only by supporters of individual accounts. As former president Bill Clinton pointed out, the only ways to keep Social Security solvent are to

1. raise taxes;
2. cut benefits; or
3. get a higher rate of return through private capital investment.

Certainly, throughout its history, Social Security taxes have been raised frequently to keep the system financially viable. The initial Social Security tax was 2 percent (split between the employer and employee), capped at $3,000 of earnings. That made for a maximum tax of $60. Since then, as Figure 7.3 shows, the payroll tax rate and the ceiling at which wages are subject to the tax have been raised a combined total of 67 times. In 2016, the tax was 12.4 percent, capped at $118,500, for a maximum tax of $14,694. Even adjusting for inflation, that represents more than an 800 percent increase.

Alternatively, Congress can reduce Social Security benefits. Restoring the program to solvency would require an immediate 16 percent cut to benefits. If reform is delayed until, say, 2034, the required cut would grow to 23 percent. Suggested changes include raising the retirement age further, trimming cost-of-living adjustments, means testing, or changing the wage-price indexing formula.

Obviously, there are better and worse ways to make these changes. But, as described above, most younger workers will receive returns far below those provided by private investment. Some will actually receive less in benefits than they pay into the system, a negative return. Both tax hikes and benefit reductions further reduce the return that workers can expect on their contributions (taxes).

Figure 7.3
Payroll Tax Rate and Taxable Maximum Increases, 1938–2013

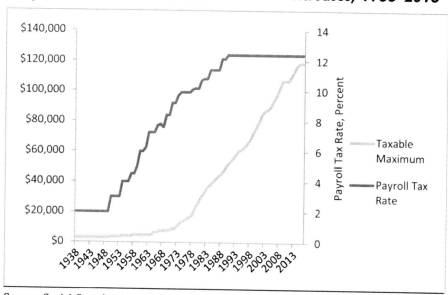

SOURCE: Social Security Administration.

Perhaps the best way to reduce Social Security benefits would be to change the formula used to calculate the initial benefit so that benefits are indexed to price inflation rather than national wage growth. Since wages tend to grow at a rate roughly one-percentage point faster than prices, such a change would hold future Social Security benefits constant in real terms but would eliminate the benefit escalation that is built into the current formula. The Congressional Budget Office estimates that this change would reduce scheduled outlays by 7 percent in 2040 and 40 percent by 2080. This reform would result in the largest reduction in the actuarial shortfall of any options that the Congressional Budget Office analyzed, representing an 80 percent improvement. Variations on this approach would apply the formula change only to higher-income seniors, preserving the current wage-indexed formula for low-income seniors.

Better Reform: Personal Accounts

Ultimately, benefit reductions or tax increases are the only ways to restore Social Security to permanent sustainable solvency. But Social Security taxes are already so high, relative to benefits, that Social Security has quite simply become a bad deal for younger workers, providing a low, below-

Table 7.2
Funded Social Security System

Generation	Period 1	Period 2	Period 3	Period 4
0	Retired	Dead	Dead	Dead
1	Working → contributions	Retired benefits	Dead	Dead
2	Unborn	Working → contributions	Retired benefits	Dead
3	Unborn	Unborn	Working → contributions	Retired benefits
4	Unborn	Unborn	Unborn	Working → contributions

SOURCE: Thomas Siems, "Reengineering Social Security for the New Economy," Cato Institute Social Security Paper no. 22, January 23, 2001.

market rate of return. It makes sense, therefore, to combine any reduction in government-provided benefits with an option for younger workers to save and invest a portion of their Social Security taxes through individual accounts.

Table 7.2 shows what that would mean. Unlike the current Social Security system, each working generation's contributions actually would be saved and would accumulate as time passes. The accumulated funds, including the returns earned through real investment, would then be used to pay that generation's benefits when they retire. Under a funded system, there would be no transfer from current workers to current retirees. Each generation pays for its own retirement.

In a funded system, there is a direct link between contributions and benefits. Each generation receives benefits equal to its contribution plus the returns the investments earn. And because real investment takes place and the rate of return on capital investment can be expected to exceed the growth in wages, workers can expect to receive higher returns than under the current system.

Moving to a system of individual accounts would allow workers to take advantage of the potentially higher returns available from capital investment. In a dynamically efficient economy, the return on capital will exceed the rate of return on labor and therefore will be higher than the benefits that Social Security can afford to pay. In the United States, the return on capital has generally run about 2.5 percentage points higher than the return on labor.

True, capital markets are both risky and volatile. But private capital investment remains remarkably safe over the long term. For example, a 2012 Cato Institute study looked at a worker retiring in 2011, near the nadir of the stock market's recession-era decline. If that worker had been allowed to invest the employee half of the Social Security payroll tax over his working lifetime, he would have retired with *more* income than if he relied on Social Security. Indeed, even in the worst-case scenario, a low-wage worker who invested entirely in bonds, the benefits from private investment would equal those from traditional Social Security. While there are limits and caveats to this type of analysis, it clearly shows that the argument that private investment is too risky compared with Social Security does not hold up.

Low-income workers would be among the biggest winners under a system of privately invested individual accounts. Private investment would pay low-income workers significantly higher benefits than can be paid by Social Security. And that does not take into account the fact that blacks, other minorities, and the poor have below-average life expectancies. As a result, they tend to live fewer years in retirement and collect less in Social Security benefits than do whites. In a system of individual accounts, they would each retain control over the funds paid in and could pay themselves higher benefits over their fewer retirement years, or leave more to their children or other heirs.

The higher returns and benefits of a private, invested system would be most important to low-income families, as they most need the extra funds. The funds saved in the individual retirement accounts, which could be left to the children of the poor, would also greatly help families break out of the cycle of poverty. Similarly, the improved economic growth, higher wages, and increased jobs that would result from an investment-based Social Security system would be most important to the poor. Without reform, low-income workers will be hurt the most by the higher taxes or reduced benefits that will be necessary if we continue on our current course.

In addition, with average- and low-wage workers accumulating large sums in their own investment accounts, the distribution of wealth throughout society would become far broader than it is today. No policy proposed in recent years would do more to expand capital ownership than allowing younger workers to invest a portion of their Social Security taxes through personal accounts. Even the lowest-paid American worker would benefit from capital investment.

Cato's Social Security Plan

- Individuals will be able to privately invest **6.2 percentage points** of their payroll tax in individual accounts. Those who choose to do so will forfeit all future accrual of Social Security benefits.
- Individuals who choose individual accounts will receive **a recognition bond** based on past contributions to Social Security. The zero coupon bonds will be offered to all workers who have contributed to Social Security, regardless of how long they have been in the system, but will be offered on a discounted basis.
- **Allowable investment options** for the individual accounts will be based on a three-tier system: a centralized, pooled collection and holding point; a limited series of investment options, with a life-cycle fund as a default mechanism; and a wider range of investment options for individuals who accumulate a minimum level in their accounts.
- At retirement, individuals will be given the **option of purchasing a family annuity or taking a programmed withdrawal.** The two options will be mandated only to the level needed to provide an income above a certain minimum. Funds in excess of the amount required to achieve that minimum level of retirement income can be withdrawn in a lump sum.
- Individuals who accumulate sufficient funds within their account to allow them to purchase an annuity that will keep them above a minimum income level in retirement will be **able to opt out** of the Social Security system in its entirety.
- **The remaining 6.2 percentage points of payroll taxes** will be used to pay transition costs and to fund disability and survivors benefits. Once, far in the future, transition costs are fully paid for, this portion of the payroll tax will be reduced to the level necessary to pay survivors and disability benefits.
- The Social Security system will be **restored to a solvent pay-as-you-go program** before individual accounts are devel-
(continued on next page)

(continued)

oped and implemented. Workers who choose to remain in the traditional Social Security system will receive whatever level of benefits Social Security can pay with existing Trust Fund levels. The best method for restoring the system's solvency is to change the initial benefit formula from wage indexing to price indexing.

Conclusion

Social Security is not sustainable without reform. Simply put, it cannot pay promised future benefits with current levels of taxation. Every year that we delay reforming the system increases the size of Social Security's shortfall and makes the inevitable changes more painful.

Raising taxes or cutting benefits will only make a bad deal worse. At the same time, workers have no ownership of their benefits, and Social Security benefits are not inheritable. That reality is particularly problematic for low-wage workers and minorities. Perhaps most important, the current Social Security system gives workers no choice or control over their financial future.

It is long past time for Congress to act.

Suggested Readings

Gokhale, Jagadeesh. *Social Security: A Fresh Look at Policy Alternatives*. Chicago, IL: University of Chicago Press, 2010.

Miron, Jeffrey. *Fiscal Imbalance: A Primer*. Washington: Cato Institute, 2015.

Pinera, Jose. "Empowering Workers: The Privatization of Social Security in Chile." *Cato's Letters* no. 10, May 1996.

Tanner, Michael. "The 6.2 Percent Solution: A Plan for Reforming Social Security." Cato Institute Social Security Paper no. 32, February 17, 2004.

———. *Going for Broke*. Washington: Cato Institute, 2015.

———. "Social Security, Ponzi Schemes, and the Need for Reform." Cato Institute Policy Analysis no. 689, November 17, 2011.

———. "Still a Better Deal: Private Investment vs. Social Security." Cato Institute Policy Analysis no. 692, February 13, 2012.

Tanner, Michael, ed. *Social Security and Its Discontents: Perspectives on Choice*. Washington: Cato Institute, 2004.

—Prepared by Michael Tanner

8. Military Budget

The United States spent $607 billion on "national defense" in 2016, according to the government's definition. That includes $522 billion for the nonwar, or base, Pentagon budget; $59 billion in the Overseas Contingency Operations (OCO) budget, ostensibly for wars; and $26 billion for defense-related activities in other agencies, principally the Department of Energy's spending on nuclear weapons. That total, hereafter referred to as the military budget (as it is not particularly defensive), is 36 percent higher in real terms than in 2000, with two-thirds of the growth in nonwar spending. That is more, in inflation-adjusted terms, than annual military spending during the Cold War, except for the brief peaks during the Korean War and the 1980s (Figure 8.1). It is more than double what Russia, China, Iran, and North Korea collectively spend on their militaries. And that amount excludes an additional $290 billion in U.S. security-related spending, which funds the budgets of Veterans Affairs, Homeland Security, and the State Department.

Still, according to the officials in the Pentagon, White House, and Congress who manage the military budget, that amount is too small, a victim of cuts required to meet the annual "sequestration caps" imposed by the 2011 Budget Control Act, in the name of deficit reduction. They argue that the caps, in place through 2021, are overly austere and threaten to leave the U.S. military underfunded and unable to meet mounting dangers. The caps remain only because of partisan disagreement over how to end them without increasing federal debt.

This chapter takes the opposite view. It argues for lowering the caps and cutting the military budget because it does not defend against national security threats so much as pursue a strategy of primacy, which amounts to trying to dominate global politics with the U.S. military. The chapter then considers alternative ways of cutting the military budget and makes the case for using the grand strategy of restraint to guide cuts. Finally, the chapter discusses specific areas of the budget to cut, as recommended under restraint.

Figure 8.1
Historical U.S. Military Spending

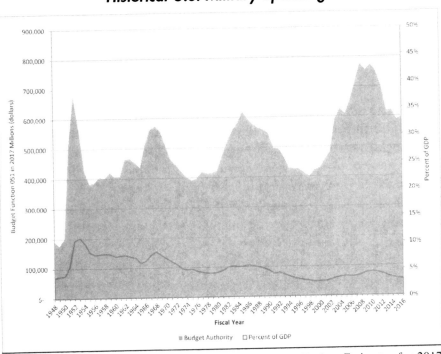

SOURCE: U.S. Department of Defense, "National Defense Budget Estimates for 2017 (Greenbook)," March 2016: http://comptroller.defense.gov/portals/45/Documents/defbudget /fy2017_Green_Book.pdf.

Why the Military Budget Should Be Cut

Before turning to the main argument—cutting the military budget— two common objections are worth addressing. One says that because the budget is economically sustainable, it should not cause concern. It is 3.3 percent of gross domestic product (GDP) and 15 percent of federal spending, which is far less than entitlement spending. Those looking to reduce deficits should find fatter targets, so the argument goes.

It is true that the U.S. military budget is economically sustainable. Thanks to economic growth, that 3.3 percent of GDP buys more than the 13 percent of GDP we spent on defense in the early 1950s. We could spend far more without economic calamity. But there is a difference between what is possible and what is wise. The United States is rich enough to do all sorts of foolish things, at least for a long time. Even so, resources remain limited, and spending frivolously takes funds from better uses. The view that defense should be spared the axe because entitlements cost more assumes either that excess can only be confronted one place at a time or that heavy spending in one place justifies waste elsewhere.

A second objection to cuts, periodically expressed by Pentagon leaders, is that the military budget has already taken its cuts thanks to the "sequestration" imposed over the last several years. That argument is misleading on two counts. First, although the 2011 Budget Control Act did impose austerity on the Pentagon via spending caps in place through fiscal year 2021, the equal, across-the-board cuts known as sequestration occurred automatically only in 2013. In each subsequent year, sequestration would have occurred only to enforce the caps if Pentagon spending exceeded them. Second, the planned cuts never quite arrived. Compliance with the original caps would have cut base spending 14 percent by 2021—hardly draconian after a decade in which it grew 40 percent. The budget deals reduced that cut from 14 percent to 10 percent, according to Congressional Research Service estimates. War funds further reduced austerity's bite. Because OCO is exempt from the caps once Congress and the president declare an "emergency," it can be used to transfer uncapped money to cover the Pentagon's nonwar needs. Congress can technically comply with the cap, avoiding sequestration, while handing the Pentagon its money back under the table through OCO. According to a recent Stimson Center report, nearly half of the OCO budget now properly belongs in the base.

Those attenuated caps did force some adjustments to Pentagon plans. Active-duty Army end-strength dropped from 570,000 to 475,000 troops over the last five years and is due to hit 450,000 in 2018 (980,000 including the National Guard and Reserves). The Navy and Air Force saw delays in the procurement of new aircraft and ships and some orders trimmed. Some administrative units shrank, and Congress finally agreed to some modest efforts to curtail pay raises and health care and housing benefits.

Still, the Pentagon dodged the hard choices that a real drawdown would have required. No cancellation of a major procurement program has occurred since 2011. More important, the Pentagon essentially avoided strategic adjustment. The much-ballyhooed rebalancing (or "pivot") to Asia produced no rebalancing of funds to the Navy and Air Force, which are most relevant to China. U.S. leaders renewed troop commitments to Europe and the Middle East. The only big change that has a strategic rationale is the Army's shrinkage.

The insufficiency of the recent cuts is evident in the Pentagon's latest five-year spending plan. According to the Congressional Budget Office

(CBO), the plan would exceed the caps by $112 billion between 2017 and 2021. Moreover, as CBO notes, less rosy assumptions about cost control and adoption of measures Congress heartily opposes (e.g., another round of Base Realignment and Closures) add another $57 billion to that excess by 2021. Congress is likely to raise budget caps again, but not enough to cover the difference. Nor is the expiration of the current caps in 2021 likely to end the search for military savings. CBO expects federal spending to raise the deficit from 2.9 to 5.0 percent of GDP over 10 years, while adding nearly $10 trillion in debt. Recent experience suggests that this debt will sustain the push for deficit controls. Republicans will likely block tax increases, Democrats will protect entitlements, and deficit-reduction efforts will focus on discretionary spending, more than half of which belongs to the Pentagon.

The primary reason that the Pentagon budget should be cut is that it is far bigger than threats to U.S. security require. Three points are worth noting here. First, U.S. wealth, technical prowess, and geography generate enviable security before the Pentagon spends a cent. The dangers that states create militaries to combat—invasion and civil war—are unthinkable here.

Second, little of the U.S. military budget is related to fighting the terrorist groups that draw so much military attention. Those costs are mostly contained within the $59 billion OCO budget. A more generous count that includes the budget for special operations and a portion of the intelligence budget still falls well short of $100 billion, or a sixth of the total budget. Even a more expansive war against the Islamic State and the various remaining al Qaeda affiliates would not require added military capability or spending in the base (nonwar) Pentagon budget—unless, that is, the United States launches another manpower-intensive counterinsurgency operation in a foreign state or two.

Third, the nations that threaten the United States are historically few and weak. North Korea remains a blustery troublemaker with a tiny nuclear arsenal and a ballistic missile arsenal of decent range. But poverty has atrophied its military capabilities to the point that its internal collapse is a bigger threat than its aggression. Iran has the money to fund extremists like Hezbollah and to antagonize its neighbors. But its military lacks the expeditionary capability to pose much direct threat to its neighbors, let alone U.S. forces, unless they are occupying Iran. The recent nuclear deal does not much affect that military balance. Russia is considerably more capable and a threat to its weak neighbors, especially Ukraine. But with an energy-dependent economy now about the size of Italy's, the Kremlin has little ability to challenge nations further west, whatever its ambitions.

Of course, in the longer term the most capable challenger to the U.S. military is China. Should it sustain its rapid growth, which is doubtful, and continue its recent rate of investment in its naval and air forces, it could become the dominant military power in East Asia and even rival the United States in some respects. That might encourage Beijing to more forcefully assert its contested claims in the East and South China Seas, heightening tensions with the United States, insofar as it backs China's local rivals. Several recent think tank studies suggest that improved Chinese surveillance and missile capability will soon threaten U.S. aircraft and ships, especially aircraft carriers, at greater distance. That capability, it is feared, will deter U.S. forces from defending allies or will embolden the Chinese to see things that way and risk aggression.

That argument should not preclude a drawdown for several reasons. One is that it overlooks countermeasures that U.S. ships can take to defend themselves. If need be, U.S. military spending can be redirected to address the problem, rather than increased overall. Two, China's ability to conquer U.S. allies will remain limited, given the inherent advantages held by those defending their own shores and their ability to adopt the same technologies abetting Chinese defensive improvements. Three, the argument overstates the difficulty of deterrence. It implies that only invulnerable forces can deter aggression, which would have surprised the Cold War architects of U.S. defenses in Germany. And it casts China's generally pragmatic leaders as zealots willing to risk economic dislocation and nuclear war for nationalistic adventures.

How to Cut Military Spending

The real reason U.S. military spending is so high is not the threats it meets but the ambitions it serves. The primacy strategy of global military dominance, fails to guide choices among military responses to danger. Because primacy sees threats and prescribes forces almost everywhere, it offers little basis for budgetary limits or prioritization. In that sense, it is less a strategy than a justification for expansive military ambitions. At a minimum, it endorses the present size of the U.S. military, with units permanently deployed in Europe, East Asia, and the Middle East, various training missions, and global naval patrols.

A strategy of restraint, by contrast, would husband U.S. power and focus planning on actual threats. By keeping U.S. forces out of avoidable troubles, restraint would reduce the number of wars the Pentagon must plan to fight, allowing big reductions in military spending. A less busy military could be a smaller and cheaper one.

Cuts guided by restraint would save far more than those offered by the most popular method of reducing spending, which is to target "waste, fraud, and abuse." As a candidate, Donald Trump claimed savings from waste, fraud, and abuse would cover the cost of his military build-up. This approach objects less to U.S. military ambitions than to the Pentagon's inefficiency in pursuing them. It recommends savings via managerial reforms—acquisition reforms, improved financial management, and empowering civilian technocrats to eliminate programs that seem redundant.

The problem with that approach is that the spending it targets is a chimera. Everyone opposes "waste." But attempts to find it reveal that nearly every military program does something and creates a political constituency who swear that the nation's security requires its full funding. The Pentagon surely spends too much buying weapons, but the trouble is rarely sneaky contractors or rules that fail to control them, so much as satisfying those who rule over acquisitions: military leaders load in requirements to serve their service's goals, and members of congressional defense committees defend the contracts that employ a chunk of their constituents. Achieving real Pentagon savings requires having fewer goals and taking on the special interests dependent on the associated spending.

A second alternative approach to cuts is the "Nike" way, in which you "just do it," lowering the total and letting the Pentagon sort out the details. That is essentially the approach that the White House and congressional leadership inadvertently selected by agreeing to spending caps while asking the Pentagon to do everything it had been doing. One virtue of legislated future caps is that they lock in future Congresses. The difficulty of overcoming the status quo protects the cuts. This method also has the advantage of being the most doable; it is easier to agree on cutting spending than on a strategic rationale for doing so.

In theory, budgetary restraint can drive efficiency and strategic restraint. Heightened resource constraints encourage service leaders to squeeze overhead costs more than instructions to find fat. Spending constraints also require more prioritization among goals, which is the essence of strategic planning. Particularly when interservice competition occurs, budgetary pressure can cause the services to debate priorities and offer alternatives to policymakers looking to limit objectives and save money. The Navy, for example, in promoting offshore methods of meeting threats, might highlight the risks of deploying U.S. ground forces to confront them and note the advantages of carrier-based airpower over land-based fighters.

The strategic and Nike methods of cutting the budget could be fruitfully combined. Restraint, in the sense of having fewer allies and wars, is possible without budget cuts; but in the absence of fiscal pressure to adjust, restraint would likely be little more than a slogan used by those doing the same old things. By articulating a strategy of restraint, imposing lower caps, and encouraging interservice competition, leaders could get the best of both approaches.

Suggested Cuts

Restraint-oriented reforms would arrive gradually as the United States exited alliances, ended wars, closed facilities, and retired forces. They would be achieved by reducing commitments and military units. Divesting force structure would allow further savings in personnel, operations and maintenance, intelligence, and real estate costs. The following cuts, once realized, would cut roughly 25 percent from current projections.

Restraint would take advantage of America's geographic position and give the Navy a larger share of the Pentagon's reduced budget. The Navy would shrink, but less than other services. Ships and submarines have access to most of the earth's surface without the need for basing rights. With gains in range and massive increases in missile and bomb accuracy, carrier-based aircraft can deliver firepower to most targets, even in those states with considerable ability to defend their coastlines. The Navy would operate as a surge force that deploys to attack shorelines or open sea lanes, rather than pointlessly patrolling peaceful areas. Divested of presence-driven requirements, the Navy could reduce the number of carriers and associated air groups it operates to eight, retire at least three amphibious assault ships, cease production of the littoral combat ship, replace the floundering F-35 program with F/A-18s, and accelerate the shrinkage of the attack submarine force. These cuts would allow additional reductions in operations and personnel costs to match the reduced fleet size.

Restraint recommends cuts to ground forces for two reasons. One is the dearth of conventional wars in which the United States might play a leading role. In the event of a conventional war on the Korean peninsula, in the Persian Gulf region, or even in Eastern Europe, wealthy U.S. allies should man the front lines. No modern Wehrmacht is poised to overcome them. The other reason is that counterterrorism is poorly served by

Suggested Cuts

Ground Forces

- Reduce active-duty Army end-strength to 360,000 or fewer soldiers.
- Reduce active Marine Corps end-strength to 145,000 or fewer.
- Cap the Army Reserves at 165,000 soldiers.
- Reduce the Army National Guard to 290,000 soldiers.
- Reduce the Special Operations Command to 40,000.
- Reduce operations and personnel costs to match reductions in ground combat units.

Navy and Air Force

- Reduce the number of carriers and associated air groups to eight.
- Retire at least three amphibious assault ships.
- Cease production of the littoral combat ship.
- End the F-35 program and buy less advanced fighter aircraft instead.
- Accelerate the shrinkage of the attack submarine force.
- Reduce the Air Force's tactical aircraft fleet (including those in the National Guard) by at least a third.
- Reduce operations and personnel costs to match reduced force size.

Nuclear Weapons

- Limit bombers and fighter aircraft to conventional (nonnuclear) missions.
- Retire intercontinental ballistic missiles.
- Cancel the new nuclear-armed cruise missile.
- Cancel upgrades to the B-61 gravity bomb.

Administration

- Consolidate or close geographic combatant commands and overseas bases.
- Reduce three- and four-star commands.
- Reduce associated contracting and civilian personnel.
- Reform maintenance and supply systems.
- Cut spending on intelligence and missile defense.
- Adopt more cost-controlling reforms for military compensation.
- Authorize another Base Realignment and Closure round at home and for foreign bases.
- Cut most Overseas Contingency Operations funding; leave only what is actually necessary to conduct the air campaign against the Islamic State.

manpower-intensive occupational wars, which rarely produce stability, let alone democracy.

U.S. policymakers should cut the active-duty Army to 360,000 or fewer soldiers, as opposed to the current plan of 450,000, and reduce the Marine

Corps' end-strength size to 145,000 rather than 182,000. Because restraint requires less frequent deployments and reduces the emphasis on deployment speed, cuts to Reserve and National Guard forces would be proportionally smaller—the Reserves would be capped at 165,000 rather than 195,000 and the National Guard would shrink to 290,000 rather than 342,000. Reduced demand for military-to-military training and fewer wars would allow Special Operations Command to cut its current size of 63,000 down to 40,000.

Restraint also recommends cutting the Air Force's air wings across active and reserve forces. Few enemies today challenge U.S. air superiority, which is why so many missions go to drones and nonstealthy aircraft with limited ability to fend off rival aircraft or surface-to-air missiles. Recent advances in aircrafts' ability to communicate, monitor targets, and precisely strike them with laser guidance and Global Positioning Systems have made each aircraft and sortie vastly more capable of destroying targets. Naval aviation, which also benefits from these gains, can bear most of the airpower load. The Air Force's tactical aircraft fleet, including those in the National Guard, should be reduced by at least a third, allowing similar reductions in support units.

Additional reductions to the Air Force budget could come from reducing its nuclear weapons spending. A credible nuclear deterrent does not require 1,900 nuclear weapons deployed on a triad of delivery vehicles—bombers, land-based intercontinental ballistic missiles, and submarine-launched ballistic missiles. The new nuclear-armed cruise missile should be cut, and upgrades to the B-61 gravity bomb should be canceled. Shifting to a submarine-based monad could yield far larger savings. Even if extended deterrence—protecting allies from aggression—requires the ability to preempt enemy nuclear forces, which is doubtful, a submarine-launched ballistic missile force could achieve that goal. Thanks to accuracy gains, conventional cruise missiles could help by destroying hardened silos and threatening enemy arsenals. It is often said that the triad is necessary to ensure that U.S. nuclear forces survive preemptive attacks and thus to deter those attacks. But no enemy can reliably track U.S. ballistic missile submarines, let alone do so with the sort of reliability required to attempt a preemptive strike against all of them. Changes in that circumstance would be detectable in time to restore another leg, and air-launched cruise missiles could be stored as a hedge.

The cuts to force structure listed above would allow additional reductions to the Pentagon's administrative costs. Additional savings could come from consolidating combatant commands, reducing three- and four-star commands, reducing associated contracting and civilian personnel, and reforming maintenance and supply systems. Spending on intelligence and missile defense could also be reduced substantially.

Independent of strategy, compensation costs—including basic pay, medical costs, housing allowances, and other benefits—need controlling. The cost of enlisted service members has virtually doubled since 2000, with compensation far exceeding comparable private-sector earnings. Service leaders and a bipartisan coterie of defense experts annually beg Congress to adopt cost-controlling reforms. Congress should accept more aggressive cost-saving proposals in these areas.

Congress should also cut down on the Pentagon's real estate spending, starting with another Base Realignment and Closure round. The Pentagon estimates that base capacity exceeds its needs by 20 percent and that the five rounds between 1988 and 2005 produced $12 billion in recurring annual savings. Additional cuts could target the Pentagon's spending on overseas base infrastructure as the United States reduces commitments abroad.

A rough estimate is that those cuts would reduce nonwar military spending by about 20 percent, to about $435 billion. Because the United States would fight fewer wars under a policy of restraint, it could also get rid of most OCO funding, leaving only the funds actually necessary to prosecute the air campaign against the Islamic State. Generously, we can call that $20 billion, resulting in another $39 billion in annual savings compared with present spending. That yields a new military budget of $455 billion, which is 25 percent lower than the present one.

If some U.S. wars and strikes continue in Afghanistan, Pakistan, Syria, Iraq, Libya, Yemen, and Somalia, we should abandon the pretense that they are an unforeseen emergency. OCO should be folded into the base Pentagon budget, as occurred in some past wars. War spending should be included under an adjusted defense spending cap, still enforced by sequestration, which should be extended to 2025 at least.

Keeping war spending uncapped encourages Congress, with the executive branch's contrivance, to stash base defense money in OCO, a habit that reduces the need for overdue reforms in the Pentagon. The current arrangement also arguably gives Pentagon leaders incentive to support wars: it lets them reap OCO's largesse. Moreover, leaving OCO spending uncapped makes its costs seem less than they are. Because distance, low costs, and safety already make U.S. wars seem nearly costless to most citizens, the wars commence with too little thought and debate. By requiring war to be paid for now, caps would make clear the tradeoffs between war and other priorities. That would spark some congressional debate as to the worth of those conflicts and slightly combat the tendency to wage war frivolously.

Proponents of current military spending argue that a restrained military budget is a radical notion that will expose Americans to danger. But what is truly radical is the idea that U.S. security requires securing rich states in perpetuity, maintaining military interventions in several poor ones simultaneously, patrolling the seas endlessly, and spending the better part of a trillion dollars a year to those ends. Given the safety the United States can enjoy if it avoids looking for conflicts to manage, the proposals here are actually cautious. They would not only save a fortune but also might even keep U.S. forces out of avoidable trouble.

Suggested Readings

Congressional Budget Office. "Long-Term Implications of the 2016 Future Years Defense Program." Congressional Budget Office Report no. 51050, January 2016.

Friedman, Benjamin H., and Justin Logan. "Why U.S. Military Spending Is 'Foolish and Sustainable.'" *Orbis* 56, no. 2 (Spring 2012).

Friedman, Benjamin H., and Christopher A. Preble. "Budgetary Savings from Military Restraint." Cato Institute Policy Analysis no. 667, September 21, 2010.

Friedman, Benjamin H., Christopher Preble, and Matt Fay. "The End of Overkill: Reassessing Nuclear Weapons Policy." Cato Institute White Paper, September 24, 2013.

Heeley, Laicie, with Anna Wheeler. "Defense Divided, Overcoming the Challenges of Overseas Contingency Operations." Washington: Stimson Center, 2016.

Herb, Jeremy. "The Sequestration Monster Myth." *Politico*, April 13, 2015.

Sapolsky, Harvey M., Eugene Gholz, and Caitlin Talmadge. *Defense Politics: The Origin of Security Policy*, 2nd ed. New York: Routledge, 2014.

—Prepared by Benjamin H. Friedman

9. Foreign Aid

Foreign aid has risen notably since the turn of this century. The United States spends $31 billion in overseas development assistance, and total aid from rich countries is now around $147 billion per year (see Figure 9.1).

Despite that increase in foreign aid, what we know about aid and development provides little reason for enthusiasm:

- There is no correlation between aid and growth.
- Aid that goes into a poor policy environment doesn't work and contributes to debt.
- Aid conditioned on market reforms has failed.
- Countries that have adopted market-oriented policies have done so because of factors unrelated to aid.
- There is a strong relationship between economic freedom and growth.

A widespread consensus has formed about those points, even among development experts who have long supported government-to-government aid. The increase in aid reflects a gap between the scholarly consensus on the limits of development assistance and the political push that has made more spending happen.

The Dismal Record of Foreign Aid

By the 1990s, the failure of conventional government-to-government aid schemes had been widely recognized and brought the entire foreign assistance process under scrutiny. For example, a Clinton administration task force conceded that "despite decades of foreign assistance, most of Africa and parts of Latin America, Asia, and the Middle East are economically worse off today than they were 20 years ago." As early as 1989, a bipartisan task force of the House Foreign Affairs Committee concluded that U.S. aid programs "no longer either advance U.S. interests abroad or promote economic development."

Multilateral aid has also played a prominent role in the post–World War II period. The World Bank, to which the United States is the

Figure 9.1
Official Development Assistance, 1960–2015

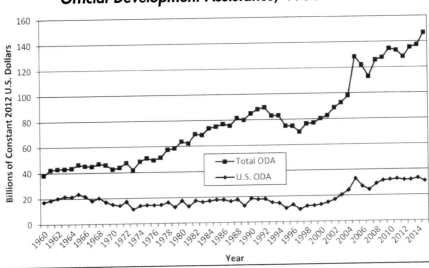

SOURCE: Organization for Economic Co-operation and Development, http://data.oecd.org/oda /net-oda.htm.

major contributor, was created in 1944 to provide aid mostly for infrastructure projects in countries that could not attract private capital on their own. The World Bank has since expanded its lending functions, as have the regional development banks that have subsequently been created on the World Bank's model and to which the United States contributes: the Inter-American Development Bank, the Asian Development Bank, the African Development Bank, and the European Bank for Reconstruction and Development. The International Monetary Fund (IMF), also established in 1944, long ago abandoned its original role of maintaining exchange-rate stability around the world and has since engaged in long-term lending on concessional terms to most of the same clients as the World Bank.

Despite record levels of lending, the multilateral development banks have not achieved any more success at promoting economic growth than has the U.S. Agency for International Development (USAID). Numerous self-evaluations of World Bank performance over the years, for example, have uncovered high failure rates of bank-financed projects. In 2000, the bipartisan congressional Meltzer Commission found a 55 to 60 percent failure rate of World Bank projects based on the bank's own evaluations. A 1998 World Bank report concluded that aid agencies "saw themselves as being primarily in the business of dishing out money, so it is not surprising that much [aid] went into poorly managed economies—with little result." The report also said that foreign aid had often been "an unmitigated failure." "No one who has seen the evidence on aid effectiveness," commented Oxford University economist Paul Collier in 1997, "can honestly say that aid is currently achieving its objective."

There are several reasons that massive transfers from the developed to the developing world have not led to a corresponding transfer of prosperity. Aid has traditionally been lent to governments, has supported central planning, and has been based on a fundamentally flawed vision of development.

By lending to governments, USAID and the multilateral development agencies supported by Washington have helped expand the state sector at the expense of the private sector in poor countries. U.S. aid to India from 1961 to 1989, for example, amounted to well over $2 billion, almost all of which went to the Indian state. Moreover, much aid goes to autocratic governments.

Foreign aid has thus financed governments, both authoritarian and democratic, whose policies have been the principal cause of their countries' impoverishment. Trade protectionism, byzantine licensing schemes, inflationary monetary policy, price and wage controls, nationalization of industries, exchange-rate controls, state-run agricultural marketing boards, and restrictions on foreign and domestic investment, for example, have all been supported explicitly or implicitly by U.S. foreign aid programs.

Not only has lack of economic freedom kept literally billions of people in poverty, but development planning has thoroughly politicized the economies of developing countries. Centralization of economic decisionmaking in the hands of political authorities has meant that a substantial amount of poor countries' otherwise useful resources has been diverted to unproductive activities, such as rent seeking by private interests or politically motivated spending by the state.

Precisely because aid operates within the (usually deficient) political and institutional environments of recipient countries, even when it goes to countries that don't rely on development planning, it can have detrimental effects. That is all the more true with higher levels of foreign assistance, as has been the case with Sub-Saharan African countries, most of which have received 10 percent or more of their national income in foreign aid for at least three decades. As Nobel laureate in economics Angus Deaton notes, "large inflows of foreign aid change local politics for the worse and undercut the institutions needed to foster long-run growth. Aid also undermines democracy and civic participation, a direct loss over and above the losses that come from undermining economic development."

It has become abundantly clear that, as long as the conditions for economic growth do not exist in developing countries, no amount of foreign aid will be able to produce economic growth. Indeed, a comprehensive study by the IMF found no relationship between aid and growth. Moreover, economic growth in poor countries does not depend on official transfers from outside sources. Were that not so, no country on earth could ever have escaped from initial poverty. The long-held premise of foreign assistance—that poor countries were poor because they lacked capital—not only ignored thousands of years of economic development history, it also was contradicted by contemporary events in the developing world, which saw the accumulation of massive debt, not development.

Promotion of Market Reforms

Even aid intended to advance market liberalization can produce undesirable results. Such aid takes the pressure off recipient governments and allows them to postpone, rather than promote, necessary but politically difficult reforms. Ernest Preeg, former chief economist at USAID, for instance, saw that problem in the Philippines after the collapse of the Marcos dictatorship: "As large amounts of aid flowed to the Aquino government from the United States and other donors, the urgency for reform dissipated. Economic aid became a cushion for postponing difficult internal decisions on reform. A central policy focus of the Aquino government became that of obtaining more and more aid rather than prompt implementation of the reform program."

Far more effective at promoting market reforms is the suspension or elimination of aid. Although USAID lists South Korea and Taiwan as success stories of U.S. economic assistance, those countries began to take off economically only after massive U.S. aid was cut off. As even the World Bank has conceded, "Reform is more likely to be preceded by a decline in aid than an increase in aid."

Still, much aid is delivered on the condition that recipient countries implement market-oriented economic policies. Such conditionality is the basis for the World Bank's structural adjustment lending, which it began in the early 1980s after it realized that pouring money into unsound economies would not lead to self-sustaining growth. But aid conditioned on reform has been ineffective at inducing reform. One 1997 World Bank study noted that there "is no systematic effect of aid on policy." A 2002 World Bank study admitted that "too often, governments receiving aid were not truly committed to reforms" and that "the Bank has often been overly optimistic about the prospects for reform, thereby contributing to misallocation of aid." Oxford's Paul Collier explains: "Some governments have chosen to reform, others to regress, but these choices appear to have been largely independent of the aid relationship. The microevidence of this result has been accumulating for some years. It has been suppressed by an unholy alliance of the donors and their critics. Obviously, the donors did not wish to admit that their conditionality was a charade."

Lending agencies have an institutional bias toward continued lending even if market reforms are not adequately introduced. Yale University economist Gustav Ranis explains that within some lending agencies, "ultimately the need to lend will overcome the need to ensure that those [loan] conditions are indeed met." In the worst cases, of course, lending agencies do suspend loans in an effort to encourage reforms. When those reforms begin or are promised, however, the agencies predictably respond by resuming the loans—a process Ranis has referred to as a "time-consuming and expensive ritual dance."

In sum, aiding reforming nations, however superficially appealing, does not produce rapid and widespread liberalization. Just as Congress should reject funding for regimes that are uninterested in reform, it should reject schemes that call for funding countries on the basis of their records of reform. This includes the Millennium Challenge Corporation, a U.S. aid agency created in 2004 to direct funds to poor countries with sound policy environments. The most obvious problem with that program is that it is based on a conceptual flaw: countries that are implementing the right policies for growth, and therefore do not need foreign aid, will be receiving aid. In practice, the effectiveness of such selective aid has been questioned by a recent IMF review that found "no evidence that aid works better in better policy or geographical environments, or that certain forms of aid work better than others."

The practical problems are indeed formidable. The Millennium Challenge Corporation and other programs of its kind require government officials and aid agencies—all of which have a poor record in determining when and where to disburse foreign aid—to make complex judgment calls on which countries deserve the aid and when. Moreover, it is difficult to believe that bureaucratic self-interest, micromanagement by Congress, and other political or geostrategic considerations will not continue to play a role in the disbursement of this kind of foreign aid. It is important to remember that the creation of the Millennium Challenge Corporation was not an attempt to reform U.S. foreign aid. Rather, the aid funds it administers are in addition to the much larger traditional aid programs that will continue to be run by USAID—in many cases in the very same countries.

Help for the Private Sector

Enterprise funds are another initiative intended to help market economies. Under this approach, the U.S. government, typically through USAID, has established and financed venture funds throughout the developing world. The purpose is to promote economic progress and "jump start" the market by investing in the private sector. Some of them have expired, some still exist, and others are being proposed.

It was never clear exactly how such government-supported funds find profitable private ventures in which the private sector is unwilling to invest. Numerous evaluations have found that most enterprise funds have lost money, and many have simply displaced private investment that otherwise would have occurred. Moreover, there is no evidence that the funds have generated additional private investment, had a positive effect on development, or helped create a better investment environment in poor countries.

Similar efforts to underwrite private entrepreneurs are evident at the World Bank (through its program to guarantee private-sector investment) and at U.S. agencies such as the Export-Import Bank, Overseas Private Investment Corporation, and the Trade and Development Agency, which provide comparable services. U.S. officials justify the programs on the grounds that they help promote development and benefit the U.S. economy. Yet providing loan guarantees and subsidized insurance to the private sector relieves the governments of underdeveloped countries of the need to create an investment environment that would attract foreign capital on its own. To attract much-needed investment, countries should establish secure property rights and sound economic policies, rather than rely on Washington-backed schemes that allow avoidance of those reforms.

Moreover, while some corporations clearly benefit from the array of foreign assistance schemes, the U.S. economy and American taxpayers do not. Subsidized loans and insurance programs amount to corporate welfare. Macroeconomic policies and conditions, not corporate welfare programs, affect factors such as the unemployment rate and the size of the trade deficit. Programs that benefit specific interest groups manage only to rearrange resources within the U.S. economy and do so in a very wasteful manner. Indeed, the United States did not achieve and does not maintain its status as the world's largest exporter because of agencies like the Export-Import Bank, which finances less than 2 percent of U.S. exports.

Even USAID has claimed that the main beneficiary of its lending is the United States because close to 80 percent of its contracts and grants go to American firms. That argument is fallacious. "To argue that aid helps the domestic economy," renowned economist Peter Bauer explained, "is like saying that a shop-keeper benefits from having his cash register burgled so long as the burglar spends part of the proceeds in his shop."

Debt Relief

By the mid-1990s, dozens of countries suffered from inordinately high foreign debt levels. Thus, the World Bank and the IMF devised a $75 billion debt-relief initiative benefiting 39 heavily indebted poor countries. The initiative, of course, is an implicit recognition of the failure of past lending to produce self-sustaining growth, especially since an overwhelming percentage of eligible countries' public foreign debt is owed to bilateral and multilateral lending agencies. Indeed, in 2006, at about the time the debt relief initiative began taking effect, 96 percent of those countries' long-term debt was public or publicly guaranteed.

Forgiving poor nations' debt is a sound idea, on the condition that no other aid is forthcoming. Unfortunately, the multilateral debt initiative promises to keep poor countries on a borrowing treadmill, since they will be eligible for future multilateral loans based on conditionality. There is no reason, however, to believe that conditionality will work any better in the future than it has in the past. Again, as a World Bank study emphasized, "A conditioned loan is no guarantee that reforms will be carried out—or last once they are."

Nor is there reason to believe that debt relief will work better now than in the past. As former World Bank economist William Easterly has documented, donor nations have been forgiving poor countries' debts since the late 1970s, and the result has simply been more debt. From 1989 to 1997, 41 highly indebted countries saw some $33 billion of debt forgiveness, yet they still found themselves in an untenable position by the time the current round of debt forgiveness began. Indeed, they have been borrowing ever-larger amounts from aid agencies. Easterly notes, moreover, that private credit to the heavily indebted poor countries has been virtually replaced by foreign aid and that foreign aid itself has been lent on increasingly easier terms.

The debt relief initiative has in fact reduced debt, but only time will tell whether this latest round of forgiveness will be yet another failed attempt to resolve poor countries' debt. Unfortunately, there are already worrying signs. For example, debt owed to official and private creditors has been rising steadily again in African countries that made up the bulk of the heavily indebted poor countries initiative. The public debt of Sub-Saharan African countries is now 35 percent of gross domestic product, up from 27 percent just four years earlier.

Other Initiatives

The inadequacy of government-to-government aid programs has prompted an increased reliance on nongovernmental organizations (NGOs). NGOs, or private voluntary organizations (PVOs), are said to be more effective at delivering aid and accomplishing development objectives because they are less bureaucratic and more in touch with the on-the-ground realities of their clients.

Although channeling official aid monies through PVOs has been referred to as a "privatized" form of foreign assistance, it is often difficult to make a sharp distinction between government agencies and PVOs beyond the fact that the latter are subject to less oversight and are less accountable. Michael Maren, a former employee at Catholic Relief Services and USAID, notes that most PVOs receive most of their funds from government sources.

Given that relationship—PVO dependence on government hardly makes them private or voluntary—Maren and others have described how the charitable goals on which PVOs are founded have been undermined. The nonprofit organization Development GAP, for example, observed that USAID's "overfunding of a number of groups has taxed their management capabilities, changed their institutional style, and made them more bureaucratic and unresponsive to the expressed needs of the poor overseas." Maren adds, "When aid bureaucracies evaluate the work of NGOs, they have no incentive to criticize them." For their part, NGOs naturally have an incentive to keep official funds flowing. The lack of proper impact assessments plagues the entire foreign aid establishment, prompting former USAID head Andrew Natsios to acknowledge, "We don't get an objective analysis of what is really going on, whether the programs are working or not." In the final analysis, government provision of foreign assistance through PVOs instead of traditional channels does not produce dramatically different results.

Microenterprise lending, another increasingly popular program among advocates of aid, is designed to provide small amounts of credit to the world's poorest people. The poor use the loans to establish livestock, manufacturing, and trade enterprises, for example. Many microloan programs, such as the one run by the Grameen Bank in Bangladesh, appear to be highly successful. Grameen has disbursed almost $20 billion since the 1970s and achieved a repayment rate of about 97 percent according to its founder. Microenterprise lending institutions, moreover, are intended to be economically viable, to achieve financial self-sufficiency within three to seven years.

Given those qualities, it is unclear why microlending organizations would require subsidies. Indeed, microenterprise banks typically refer to themselves as profitable enterprises. For those and other reasons, Jonathan Morduch of New York University concluded in a 1999 study that "the greatest promise of microfinance is so far unmet, and the boldest claims do not withstand close scrutiny." He added that, according to some estimates, "if subsidies are pulled and costs cannot be reduced, as many as 95 percent of current programs will eventually have to close shop." More recently, David Roodman of the Center for Global Development found little evidence for the grand claims of the microcredit movement, including that it can noticeably reduce poverty. He advocated reducing funding for microlending and increasing its effectiveness.

Furthermore, microenterprise programs alleviate the conditions of the poor, but they do not address the causes of the lack of credit faced by the poor. In developing countries, for example, about 90 percent of poor people's property is not recognized by the state. Without secure private property rights, most of the world's poor cannot use collateral to obtain a loan. The Institute for Liberty and Democracy, a Peruvian think tank, found that, when poor people's property in Peru was registered, new businesses were created, production increased, asset values rose by 200 percent, and credit became available. Of course, the scarcity of credit is also caused by a host of other policy measures, such as financial regulation that makes it prohibitively expensive to provide banking services for the poor.

In sum, microenterprise programs can be beneficial, but successful programs need not receive aid subsidies. The success of microenterprise programs, moreover, will depend on specific conditions, which vary greatly from country to country. For that reason, microenterprise projects should be financed privately by people who have their own money at stake rather than by international aid bureaucracies that appear intent on replicating such projects throughout the developing world.

Conclusion

Numerous studies have found that economic growth is strongly related to the level of economic freedom. Put simply, the greater a country's economic freedom, the greater its level of prosperity over time (Figure 9.2). Likewise, the greater a country's economic freedom, the faster it will grow. Economic freedom—which includes not only policies, such as free trade and stable money, but also institutions, such as the rule of law and the security of private property rights—increases more than just income. It is also strongly related to improvements in other development indicators such as longevity, access to safe drinking water, lower corruption, and dramatically higher incomes for the poorest members of society (Figure 9.3).

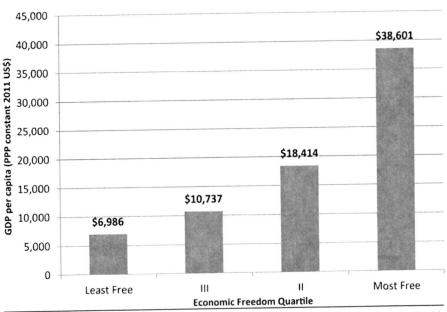

Figure 9.2
Economic Freedom and Income per Capita, 2013

SOURCE: James Gwartney, Robert Lawson, and Joshua Hall, *Economic Freedom of the World: 2015 Annual Report* (Vancouver: Fraser Institute, 2015), p. 23.

NOTE: GDP = gross domestic product; PPP = purchasing power parity.

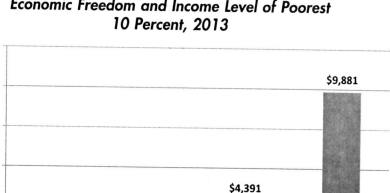

Figure 9.3
Economic Freedom and Income Level of Poorest
10 Percent, 2013

SOURCE: Gwartney James, Robert Lawson, and Joshua Hall, *Economic Freedom of the World: 2015 Annual Report* (Vancouver: Fraser Institute, 2015), p. 23.
NOTE: PPP = purchasing power parity.

The developing countries that have most liberalized their economies and achieved high levels of growth have done far more to reduce poverty and improve their citizens' standards of living than have foreign aid programs. As Deaton observes:

> Even in good environments, aid compromises institutions, it contaminates local politics, and it undermines democracy. If poverty and underdevelopment are primarily consequences of poor institutions, then by weakening those institutions or stunting their development, large aid flows do exactly the opposite of what they are intended to do. It is hardly surprising then that, in spite of the direct effects of aid that are often positive, the record of aid shows no evidence of any overall beneficial effect.

In the end, a country's progress depends almost entirely on its domestic policies and institutions, not on outside factors such as foreign aid. As Easterly suggests, aid distracts from what really matters, "such as the role of political and economic freedom in achieving development." Congress should recognize that foreign aid has not caused the worldwide shift toward the market and that appeals for more foreign aid, even when intended to promote the market, will continue to do more harm than good.

Suggested Readings

Anderson, Robert E. *Just Get Out of the Way: How Government Can Help Business in Poor Countries.* Washington: Cato Institute, 2004.

Bandow, Doug, and Ian Vásquez, eds. *Perpetuating Poverty: The World Bank, the IMF, and the Developing World.* Washington: Cato Institute, 1994.

Bauer, P. T. *Dissent on Development.* Cambridge, MA: Harvard University Press, 1972.

Deaton, Angus. *The Great Escape: Health, Wealth, and the Origins of Inequality.* Princeton: Princeton University Press, 2013.

De Soto, Hernando. *The Mystery of Capital: Why Capitalism Triumphs in the West and Fails Everywhere Else.* New York: Basic Books, 2000.

Dichter, Thomas. "A Second Look at Microfinance: The Sequence of Growth and Credit in Economic History." Cato Institute Development Briefing Paper no. 1, February 15, 2007.

Djankov, Simeon, Jose Montalvo, and Marta Reynal-Querol. "Does Foreign Aid Help?" *Cato Journal* 26, no. 1 (Winter 2006).

Easterly, William. "Freedom versus Collectivism in Foreign Aid." In *Economic Freedom of the World: 2006 Annual Report,* edited by James Gwartney and Robert Lawson. Vancouver, British Columbia: Fraser Institute, 2006, pp. 29–41.

———. *The Tyranny of Experts: Economists, Dictators, and the Forgotten Rights of the Poor.* New York: Basic Books, 2013.

———. *The White Man's Burden: Why the West's Efforts to Aid the Rest Have Done So Much Ill and So Little Good.* New York: Penguin Press, 2006.

Erixon, Fredrik. *Aid and Development: Will It Work This Time?* London: International Policy Network, 2005.

Gwartney, James, Robert Lawson, and Joshua Hall. *Economic Freedom of the World: 2016 Annual Report.* Vancouver, British Columbia: Fraser Institute, 2016.

International Financial Institution Advisory Commission (Meltzer Commission). "Report to the U.S. Congress and the Department of the Treasury." March 8, 2000.

Lal, Deepak. *The Poverty of "Development Economics."* London: Institute of Economic Affairs, 1983, 1997.

Maren, Michael. *The Road to Hell: Foreign Aid and International Charity.* New York: Free Press, 1997.

Munk, Nina. *The Idealist: Jeffrey Sachs and the Quest to End Poverty.* New York: Anchor Books, 2013.

Roodman, David. *Due Diligence: An Impertinent Inquiry into Microfinance.* Baltimore, MD: Brookings Institution Press, 2012.

Vásquez, Ian. "Commentary." In *Making Aid Work,* by Abhijit Banerjee. Cambridge, MA: MIT Press, 2007, pp. 47–53.

———. "The Asian Crisis: Why the IMF Should Not Intervene." *Vital Speeches,* April 15, 1998.

———. "The New Approach to Foreign Aid: Is the Enthusiasm Warranted?" Cato Institute Foreign Policy Briefing no. 79, September 17, 2003.

Vásquez, Ian, and John Welborn. "Reauthorize or Retire the Overseas Private Investment Corporation?" Cato Institute Foreign Policy Briefing no. 78, September 15, 2003.

—Prepared by Ian Vásquez

10. Earned Income Tax Credit

The earned income tax credit (EITC) is a large federal aid program administered through the income tax system. Benefits are available to households with earnings from employment. In 2015, the program provided $69 billion in benefits to 28 million recipients.

The EITC is partly a tax-cut program but mainly a spending program. It is "refundable," meaning that individuals who pay no income taxes are nonetheless eligible to receive payments. About $60 billion of the benefits in 2015 were refundable.

The EITC has a high error and fraud rate, and for most recipients, it creates a disincentive to increase earnings. Also, the refundable or spending part of the EITC imposes a large cost on other people who pay the taxes to fund the benefits.

Growth of the EITC

In the 1970s, policymakers considered ways to reduce the anti-work effects of the growing welfare state. One way would have been to cut the size of the welfare state, but policymakers instead decided to expand it by enacting the EITC in 1975. Initially, the program was a 10 percent wage credit with a maximum value of $400. Only workers with children were eligible.

Over the decades, Congress expanded the size and scope of the EITC. Today, it has credit rates up to 45 percent and a maximum value of $6,269 in 2016. It provides benefits to workers with and without children.

EITC expansions in 1986, 1990, 1993, and 2009 increased the program's cost. Total benefits in constant 2015 dollars increased from $14 billion in 1990, to $45 billion in 2000, to $69 billion in 2015. The number of recipients soared from 12.5 million in 1990 to 28 million in 2015.

Structure of the EITC

EITC benefits vary depending on the number of children, income level, and filing status (single or married). Initially, the credit rises with income (the phase-in range). Then the credit reaches the maximum amount and is constant for a certain range (the flat range). Finally, the credit falls as income rises further (the phase-out range).

Consider a single parent with two children in 2016. The maximum credit would be $5,572 if the parent earned between $13,931 and $18,190. Above that, the credit would phase out and then be eliminated when earnings topped $44,648. The phase-out rate is 21.06 percent, so during the phase-out range, the parent loses $210 in EITC benefits for every additional $1,000 earned. The pattern of benefits—rising, flat, then falling—is similar for other types of families.

EITC Reduces Market Wages

The EITC is supposed to strengthen work incentives for lower-income individuals. If the EITC is successful, it should increase the labor supply of low earners. On a simple supply-and-demand diagram, the labor supply curve thus shifts to the right, which tends to reduce market wages.

A growing labor supply and falling market wages induce employers to hire additional workers. Workers who receive the EITC are better off than before with the combination of a lower market wage and the EITC. But it is interesting to note that proponents of the EITC implicitly favor cutting market wages for low earners.

One side effect of the EITC is that, to the extent it works by pushing down market wages, it hurts low earners who receive either no EITC or just a small EITC. The labor-supply effect of the EITC also means that the program acts as a subsidy to businesses that hire lower-skilled workers because they are able to pay reduced market wages.

Work Incentives and Disincentives

The EITC affects work incentives in two ways. First, it affects *labor force participation*, or the incentive for nonworkers to gain employment. Second, it affects the *number of hours worked* by people who are working. The EITC affects these factors in different ways for different people, creating both positive and negative effects.

People within the EITC's income range have an added incentive to find a job because the credit increases the reward for working. Most economists think that the EITC particularly encourages low-income single mothers to join the labor force, and there is solid empirical support for that positive effect.

However, there is doubt about the strength of this effect. EITC supporters point to gains in labor force participation among single mothers in the 1990s as evidence of the credit's benefits. The number of EITC recipients soared between 1987 and 1994 but was flat in the late 1990s. Yet from 1994 forward, participation by single mothers grew strongly. So other factors, aside from the EITC, probably caused that late-1990s increase—perhaps the strong economy at the time and welfare reforms that increased work requirements.

For workers already in the labor force, the EITC creates a mix of incentives to either increase or decrease hours worked. Workers face an "income effect," which may cause some individuals to reduce work because the EITC allows them to meet their income needs with less work. Workers also face a "substitution effect," meaning that the EITC makes working more valuable compared with not working. The substitution effect varies depending on whether individuals are in the phase-in, flat, or phase-out range of the EITC. As a result, people may respond to the credit by working either more or less at different income levels. People have an incentive to reduce hours worked in both the flat and phase-out ranges of the credit, and about three-quarters of people taking the EITC are in those two ranges. So a large majority of people taking the EITC have an incentive to work less, not more.

The EITC is only one of many government programs that alter work incentives. A study by Elaine Maag and colleagues in the *National Tax Journal* examined work incentives on a hypothetical low-income single parent with two children in each of the 50 states. As this mother's earnings rise, she pays more payroll taxes and possibly more income taxes, and she receives reduced benefits from the EITC, food stamps, and Temporary Assistance for Needy Families.

On average, across the states, the Maag study found that the parent would face a marginal tax rate of about 50 percent in moving from a poverty level of income to twice the poverty level. Adding in the effects of reduced Medicaid and Affordable Care Act subsidies further reduces incentives for people to increase their market earnings.

Errors and Fraud

The EITC has a high rate of improper payments—caused by math errors, misunderstanding of the rules, and fraud. The Internal Revenue Service reported that the EITC error and fraud rate in 2014 was 27 percent, which amounted to $18 billion in overpayments.

People are receiving excess EITC payments based on false information about such items as their income level, filing status, and qualifying children. The EITC is an easy target for dishonest filers because it is refundable, meaning that people can simply file false tax returns and wait for the Treasury to send them a check.

Part of the problem is that the EITC is complex. Benefits change as income rises, and it has multiple phase-in and phase-out rates. It is adjusted by filing status and number of children. The rules regarding child eligibility are complex due to issues such as separation and divorce. EITC rules are so complicated that two-thirds of all tax returns claiming the EITC are done by paid preparers. The credit generates so many errors that 39 percent of all IRS audits under the individual income tax are done on EITC filers.

The EITC error and fraud problems have persisted for decades, despite efforts to fix them. This is one good reason to cut or end the EITC. It is unfair to the taxpayers who fund the program for the government to misspend so much of their money year after year.

High Cost on Taxpayers

The EITC is mainly a spending program. Most payments—$60 billion a year, or 88 percent of the benefits—go to people who owe no income tax. Every dollar of those benefits is a dollar of loss for the people who pay the taxes to support the program.

Extracting those taxes to pay for the EITC damages the economy because it causes people to reduce their productive activities, such as working and investing. This economic damage is called "deadweight losses." For the federal income tax, studies have found that the deadweight loss of raising taxes by a dollar is roughly 50 cents.

Suppose that Congress expands EITC spending by $10 billion. Does the expansion make any economic sense? The benefits would have to be higher than the total cost of about $15 billion, which includes the $10 billion direct cost to taxpayers plus another $5 billion or so in deadweight losses.

EITC supporters often say that the program pulls 6 million or so people out of poverty. But that is a meaningless statistic. If the government gives low-income individuals $60 billion, of course they will have more money in their pockets, and fewer of them will be below a measured poverty line.

Why not double or triple EITC benefits and try to pull even more people out of poverty? The answer is that we need to worry about the costs of federal programs, which are the harms done to other citizens and the broader economy. Expanding the EITC would create more fraud, higher deadweight losses, and added disincentives to increase hours worked in the phase-out range.

Reform Options

The EITC should not be expanded, as some policymakers are proposing. Instead, the EITC should be cut, by reining in benefit levels and narrowing eligibility. At the same time, policymakers should pursue other policies to increase market wages and job opportunities. For example, cutting the corporate income tax rate would boost business capital investment. In turn, that would create higher demand for labor, thus generating more jobs and raising wages for all workers.

Suggested Readings

Edwards, Chris, and Veronique de Rugy. "Earned Income Tax Credit: Small Benefits, Large Costs." Cato Institute Tax and Budget Bulletin no. 73, October 2015.

Eissa, Nada, and Hilary Hoynes. "Redistribution and Tax Expenditures: The Earned Income Tax Credit." National Bureau of Economic Research Working Paper no. 14307, September 2008.

Internal Revenue Service. *Compliance Estimates for the Earned Income Tax Credit Claimed on 2006–2008 Returns.* Research, Analysis & Statistics Report, Publication 5162. Washington: Department of the Treasury, August 2014.

Maag, Elaine, C. Eugene Steuerle, Ritadhi Chakravarti, and Caleb Quakenbush. "How Marginal Tax Rates Affect Families at Various Levels of Poverty." *National Tax Journal* 65, no. 4 (December 2012): 759–82.

Mead, Lawrence M. "Overselling the Earned Income Tax Credit." *National Affairs.* Fall 2014.

Nichols, Austin, and Jesse Rothstein. "The Earned Income Tax Credit (EITC)." National Bureau of Economic Research Working Paper no. 21211, May 2015.

—Prepared by Chris Edwards

11. Infrastructure Investment

The importance of infrastructure investment to the U.S. economy is widely recognized. But policy discussions usually focus on the level of spending and ignore the efficiency by which investment is allocated and projects are built and operated. Efficiency and innovation would increase if the federal role were reduced. State and local governments and the private sector are more likely to make sound infrastructure decisions without federal intervention.

Government Infrastructure in Perspective

The word "infrastructure" refers to long-lived fixed assets that provide a backbone for other activities in the economy. In the United States, most infrastructure is provided by the private sector, not governments. In 2015, gross fixed private nonresidential investment was $2.3 trillion, according to the Bureau of Economic Analysis. That includes investment in factories, freight rail, pipelines, refineries, power plants, cell towers, satellites, and many other items.

By contrast, total federal, state, and local government infrastructure investment in 2015 was $613 billion. Excluding national defense, government investment was $472 billion. Thus private infrastructure investment—broadly defined—is about five times as large as total nondefense government investment in infrastructure.

One implication of the data is that if policymakers want to strengthen the nation's infrastructure, they should enact reforms that spur private investment. In particular, they should consider reductions in regulations and business tax rates, which would increase the net returns to a broad range of private infrastructure and thus spur greater investment spending.

Government investment in infrastructure, though smaller than private, is nevertheless important to the economy, and we should ensure that it is adequately funded. Many pundits say that America is underinvesting in public infrastructure and that our highways and bridges are crumbling. Such claims are off base. For one thing, government investment as a share of gross domestic product in the United States is similar to the average share among nations in the Organization for Economic Cooperation and Development (OECD). Over the past three years, the U.S. and OECD averages have both been 3.4 percent.

Also, rather than crumbling, some of our public infrastructure has steadily improved. Federal Highway Administration (FHWA) data on bridges show steady gains. Of the roughly 600,000 bridges in the country, the share that are "structurally deficient" has fallen from 22 percent in 1992 to 10 percent in 2015, while the share that are "functionally obsolete" has fallen from 16 percent to 14 percent.

Similarly, the surface quality of the interstate highways has improved. Examining FHWA data, Federal Reserve of Chicago economists found that "since the mid-1990s, our nation's interstate highways have become indisputably smoother and less deteriorated." They concluded that the interstate system is "in good shape relative to its past condition."

Nonetheless, America does face infrastructure challenges. Highway congestion imposes a large cost on the economy. Highways and bridges are aging. Our airports and seaports need investments to meet rising demands. State and local governments and the private sector—not the federal government—can best address these challenges.

Problems with Federal Intervention

There are frequent calls for increased federal spending on infrastructure, but advocates ignore the inefficiencies and failures of past federal efforts. Here are some of the problems:

- **Investment is misallocated.** Federal investments are often based on pork-barrel and bureaucratic factors rather than marketplace demands. Amtrak investment, for example, is spread around to low-population regions where passenger rail makes no economic sense. Lawmakers all want an Amtrak route through their state, so investment gets steered away from where it is really needed, such as the Northeast corridor.
- **Infrastructure is utilized inefficiently.** Government infrastructure is often used inefficiently because supply and demand are not balanced by market prices. The vast water infrastructure operated by the Bureau of Reclamation, for example, underprices irrigation water in the western United States. The result is wasted resources, harm to the environment, and a looming water crisis in many areas in the West.
- **Projects are mismanaged.** Unlike private businesses, governments don't have strong incentives to ensure that projects are constructed

efficiently. Federally funded highway, transit, airport, and air traffic control projects often have large cost overruns. The budget for the "Big Dig" in Boston—which was two-thirds funded by the federal government—exploded to five times the original cost estimate. And over the decades, the Army Corps of Engineers and Bureau of Reclamation have built numerous projects that were economic and environmental boondoggles.

- **Mistakes are replicated across the nation.** When Washington makes infrastructure mistakes, it replicates them across the nation. High-rise public housing projects, for example, were a terrible idea that federal funding spread nationwide. More recently, federal subsidies for light-rail projects have biased cities in favor of these expensive systems, even though they are generally less efficient and flexible than bus systems.
- **Burdensome regulations.** Federal infrastructure aid comes part and parcel with costly regulations. Federal Davis-Bacon rules raise the labor costs of building state and local infrastructure. The rules inflate wages on highway projects by about one-fifth. Federal environmental rules also impose costs on transportation projects. The number of environmental laws affecting transportation projects has risen from about 20 in 1970 to about 70 today, according to the FHWA.

The solution to these problems is to privatize federally owned infrastructure, cut federal aid to the states, and reduce federal regulations so that the states can tackle their infrastructure challenges in the most efficient manner.

Privatizing Federal Infrastructure

A privatization revolution has swept the world since the 1980s. Governments in more than 100 countries have transferred thousands of state-owned businesses worth more than $3 trillion to the private sector. Railroads, airports, seaports, energy utilities, and other infrastructure businesses have been privatized.

Despite the global success of privatization, reforms have largely bypassed our own federal government. Infrastructure that has been privatized abroad remains in government hands in this country. Congress should study foreign reforms and privatize the following infrastructure assets:

- **Air traffic control.** The Federal Aviation Administration has struggled to modernize our air traffic control (ATC) system. ATC is a high-technology industry, but we still run it as an old-fashioned bureaucracy. Meanwhile, Canada privatized its ATC system in 1996 as a self-funded nonprofit corporation. Today, the Canadian system is highly efficient and one of the safest in the world. The Canadians are on the leading edge of ATC technologies, and they sell their innovations worldwide.

- **Tennessee Valley Authority.** One of the largest utilities in the nation is owned by the federal government. The Tennessee Valley Authority (TVA) has a bloated cost structure and a poor environmental record, and it has wasted billions of dollars on its nuclear program. Electric utilities have been privatized around the world, so privatizing TVA should be a no-brainer.

- **Amtrak.** The government's passenger rail company has a costly union workforce and a poor on-time record, and it loses more than a billion dollars a year. A lot of the losses come from running trains on routes with low ridership. Congress should privatize Amtrak and give entrepreneurs a crack at creating a better system.

- **Power Marketing Administrations.** The federal government owns four Power Marketing Administrations (PMAs), which transmit wholesale electricity in 33 states. The power is mainly generated by hydroelectric plants owned by the Army Corps of Engineers and the Bureau of Reclamation. The PMAs receive numerous subsidies and sell most of their power at below-market rates. Congress should privatize the PMAs and the hydro plants.

- **Army Corps of Engineers.** The civilian part of the Army Corps constructs and maintains water infrastructure such as locks, waterways, and flood control structures. But the Corps is filling roles that private engineering and construction companies could fill. When the states need to construct and maintain levees, harbors, beaches, inland waterways, and recreational areas, they should hire private companies to do the work. The Army Corps should be privatized and compete for such work.

- **Bureau of Reclamation.** This agency builds and operates dams, canals, and hydro plants in the 17 Western states. It is the largest wholesaler of water in the nation. Reclamation subsidizes irrigation water, which distorts the economy and causes environmental harm. The agency's facilities should be transferred to state ownership or privatized.

States Should Lead on Infrastructure

When considering investments in highways and transit, people often assume that Washington needs to lead the effort. Many advocates support raising the federal gas tax to fund more highway and transit spending.

106

However, the nation's interstate highways, other highways, bridges, and transit systems are virtually all owned by state and local governments. The states can raise their own gas taxes to fund their transportation facilities anytime they want. Indeed, about half the states have raised their gas taxes or other transportation revenues over the past five years.

Furthermore, state governments have other options to finance their infrastructure. A growing trend around the world is partial privatization of infrastructure through public-private partnerships (P3s). P3s differ from traditional government contracting by shifting elements of financing, management, operations, and project risks to the private sector.

Infrastructure P3s have many advantages. When private businesses are taking some of the risks and putting their profits on the line, funding is more likely to be allocated to high-return projects and completed in an efficient manner. U.S. and foreign empirical studies find that privately financed infrastructure projects are more likely than traditional government projects to be completed on time and on budget.

Another issue is that the usual process of government contracting decouples construction from the future management of facilities. As a result, contractors have no incentive to build projects that minimize long-term costs. P3s solve this problem because the same company both builds and operates new facilities. Another advantage of P3s is that businesses can tap capital markets to build capacity and meet market demands—thus avoiding the instability of government budgeting.

P3s are a global trend, but the United States lags Australia, Canada, and other nations in pursuing this innovative approach. Nonetheless, some U.S. states have pursued P3s. In Virginia, a private partnership built and is now operating toll lanes along 14 miles of the Capital Beltway, I-495. The partnership used debt and equity to finance most of the project's $2 billion cost. The lanes were completed on time and on budget in 2012.

P3s are a means to partially privatize, but full privatization is also possible for some infrastructure. In Virginia, the Dulles Greenway is a privately owned toll highway completed in the mid-1990s with $350 million of private debt and equity. Also in Virginia, the FIGG Engineering Group financed and constructed the $142 million Jordan highway bridge over the Elizabeth River. The bridge opened in 2012, and investors are being paid back over time from toll revenues.

Unfortunately, such private infrastructure projects are rare in the United States. Consider that dozens of major airports around the world have been privatized, yet virtually all commercial airports in this country are owned by state and local governments. A key problem is that the federal government creates barriers to state and local privatization.

Removing Barriers to State and Local Privatization

Despite the benefits of private infrastructure, federal policies create hurdles to private sector investments. Congress should address the following issues:

- **Tax exemption on municipal bond interest.** When state and local governments borrow funds to build infrastructure, the interest on the debt is tax free under federal income tax rules. That allows governments to finance infrastructure at a lower cost than private businesses can, which stacks the deck against the private provision of facilities such as airports. Congress should repeal the tax exemption on state and local bond interest to level the playing field.
- **Federal subsidies.** Federal subsidies tilt state and local lawmakers in favor of government provision of infrastructure. Private airports, for example, are generally not eligible for federal airport subsidies. Or consider urban transit. Before the 1960s, most bus and rail services in America were privately owned and operated. But that ended with the passage of the Urban Mass Transportation Act of 1964. That act provided subsidies only to government-owned bus and rail systems, not private systems. The change prompted governments across the country to take over private systems, ending more than a century of private transit in our cities. Congress should end federal aid for state and local infrastructure.
- **Federal regulations.** Various federal regulations restrict state and local privatization. For example, states that have received federal aid for their facilities are generally required to repay the past aid if facilities are privatized. Another issue is that tolling is generally prohibited on existing interstate highways, a ban that has reduced the scope for P3 projects. Congress should eliminate these and other regulations that stand in the way of infrastructure privatization.

To conclude, America should strive for top-notch infrastructure in order to compete in the global economy. The best way forward is to reduce federal intervention and devolve control over infrastructure to the states and private sector. The states themselves should innovate with P3s and full privatization. Governments should encourage entrepreneurs to enter the fray with new ideas for meeting the nation's infrastructure demands.

Suggested Readings

Boskin, Michael J. "All Aboard the Infrastructure Boondoggle." *Wall Street Journal*, November 1, 2016.

Bureau of Economic Analysis. "National Income and Product Accounts." Table 1.5.5: Gross Domestic Product. Washington: Department of Commerce, 2016.

Campbell, Jeffrey R., and Thomas N. Hubbard. "The State of Our Interstates." Federal Reserve Bank of Chicago, Chicago Fed Letter no. 264, July 2009.

Edwards, Chris. "Cutting the Army Corps of Engineers." Cato Institute, DownsizingGovern ment.org, March 1, 2012.

———. "Options for Federal Privatization and Reform Lessons from Abroad." Cato Institute Policy Analysis no. 794, June 28, 2016.

Edwards, Chris, and Peter J. Hill. "Cutting the Bureau of Reclamation and Reforming Water Markets." DownsizingGovernment.org, Cato Institute, February 1, 2012.

Edwards, Chris, and Nicole Kaeding. "Federal Government Cost Overruns." DownsizingGovern ment.org, Cato Institute, September 1, 2015.

Federal Highway Administration. "Deficient Bridges by Highway System." *Bridges and Structures*. Washington: Department of Transportation, July 14, 2016.

Glaeser, Edward L. "If You Build It . . . Myths and Realities about America's Infrastructure Spending." *City Journal* (Summer 2016).

Poole, Robert, and Chris Edwards. "Privatizing U.S. Airports." Cato Institute Tax and Budget Bulletin no. 76, November 2016.

—Prepared by Chris Edwards

12. Fiscal Federalism

The federal government has developed a complex financial relationship with state and local governments through the grants-in-aid system. The system has grown for more than a century as the federal government has increasingly intervened in state and local activities. Today there are more than 1,100 different federal aid programs for the states. Each program has its own rules and regulations, and the overall system is a complicated mess.

It was not supposed to be this way. Under the U.S. Constitution, the federal government was assigned specific, limited powers, and most government functions were left to the states. To ensure that people understood the limits on federal power, the nation's Founders added the Constitution's Tenth Amendment: "The powers not delegated to the United States by the Constitution, nor prohibited by it to the States, are reserved to the States respectively, or to the people."

The Tenth Amendment embodies federalism, the idea that federal and state governments have separate areas of activity and that federal responsibilities are "few and defined," as James Madison noted. Historically, federalism acted as a safeguard of American freedoms. President Ronald Reagan noted in Executive Order 12612, "Federalism is rooted in the knowledge that our political liberties are best assured by limiting the size and scope of the national government."

Unfortunately, policymakers and the courts have mainly discarded federalism in recent decades. Congress has undertaken many activities that had been reserved to the states and the people. Grants-in-aid are a key mechanism that the federal government has used to extend its control. Grant programs are subsidies that come bundled with federal regulations to micromanage state and local activities.

The federal government will spend almost $700 billion on aid to the states in 2017, making it the largest item in the federal budget after Social Security. Some of the major federal aid programs are for education, health care, housing, and transportation.

There are few, if any, real advantages of federalizing state and local activities through aid programs, but many disadvantages. The aid system

111

encourages excessive spending and bureaucratic waste, reduces political accountability, and stifles policy diversity and innovation. With the ongoing flood of red ink in Washington, now would be a great time to cut the overgrown grants-in-aid system.

Brief History of Federal Aid

Prior to the Civil War, proposals to subsidize state and local activities were occasionally introduced in Congress, but they were routinely voted down or vetoed by presidents. The resistance to federal funding of state activities started to weaken toward the end of the 19th century. The Morrill Act of 1862 provided grants of federal land to the states for the establishment of colleges that focused on agriculture, mechanical studies, and the military. This was the first grant program with "strings attached." It included detailed rules for recipients to follow and required them to submit regular reports to the federal government.

Federal aid activity increased substantially in the early 20th century. When the income tax was introduced in 1913, it provided the means for policymakers to finance a range of new federal aid programs. There was resistance to the expansion of federal aid, but it was politically difficult for states to opt out of new programs. If they opted out, their residents would still have to pay federal taxes to support federal aid spending in other states.

Various sleights of hand were used to get around constitutional barriers to federal intervention in state and local affairs. For example, a 1916 law that created a broad-based federal program for road subsidies was premised on the constitutional power to fund "post roads," or roads used for mail delivery. Federal aid to schools and airports was originally justified on military grounds.

The number of grant-in-aid programs increased steadily from the 1920s to the 1950s and then exploded during the 1960s. Under President Lyndon Johnson, aid programs were added for housing, urban renewal, education, health care, and many other activities. The number of aid programs quadrupled from 132 in 1960 to 530 by 1970.

Policymakers were optimistic that federal experts and federal money could solve complex local problems such as urban decay. But as the failures of aid began to mount, the optimism faded. President Richard Nixon argued that federal aid was a "terrible tangle" of overlap and inefficiency. In his 1971 State of the Union address, he lambasted "the idea that a bureaucratic elite in Washington knows best what is best for people everywhere," and said that he wanted to "reverse the flow of power and resources from the states and communities to Washington." For his part, President Jimmy Carter proposed a "concentrated attack on red tape and confusion in the federal grant-in-aid system." Unfortunately, Nixon and Carter made little progress on reforms.

President Ronald Reagan had more success at sorting out the "confused mess" of federal aid, as he called it. In a 1981 budget law, dozens of grant programs were eliminated and many others were consolidated. Unfortunately, Reagan's progress at trimming federal aid was reversed after he left office, and there have been few efforts to cut the aid system since then. The number of aid programs has more than tripled from 335 in 1985 to more than 1,100 today.

Eight Reasons to Cut Aid

The theory behind grants-in-aid is that the federal government can create subsidy programs in the national interest to efficiently solve local problems. The belief is that policymakers can dispassionately allocate large sums of money across hundreds of activities according to a rational plan designed in Washington.

The federal aid system does not work that way in practice. Federal politicians do not have the knowledge to design programs that maximize net benefits on a national basis, and they put most of their efforts into grabbing subsidies for their own states. At the state level, federal aid stimulates overspending and creates a web of top-down rules that destroy innovation. Officials at all levels of the aid system focus mainly on spending and regulations, not on delivering quality services.

The following are eight reasons that the federal aid system does not make economic or practical sense and ought to be cut and eventually eliminated.

1. There is no magical source of federal funds. Aid supporters bemoan a "lack of resources" at the state level and believe that Uncle Sam has endlessly deep pockets to help out. But every dollar of federal aid sent to the states is ultimately taken from federal taxpayers who live in the 50 states. It is true that the federal government has a greater ability to run deficits than state governments, but that is an argument against the aid system, not in favor of it. By moving the funding of state activities to the federal level, the aid system has tilted American government toward unsustainable deficit financing.

2. Aid spurs wasteful spending. The basic incentive structure of aid programs encourages overspending by federal and state policymakers. Policymakers at both levels can claim credit for spending on a program, while relying on the other level of government to collect part of the tax bill.

Also, aid programs often include features such as matching that prompt the states to increase spending. A typical match is 50 percent, which means that for every $2 million a state expands a program, the federal government chips in $1 million. Matching reduces the "price" of states' added spending, thus prompting them to expand programs. The largest aid program, Medicaid, is a matching program.

One way to reduce the incentive to spend is to convert open-ended matching grants to block grants. Block grants provide a fixed sum to each state and allow greater program flexibility. An example of such a reform was the 1996 welfare overhaul, which turned Aid to Families with Dependent Children (an open-ended matching grant) into Temporary Assistance for Needy Families (a lump-sum block grant). Similar reforms should be pursued for Medicaid and other programs. Converting programs to block grants would reduce incentives for states to overspend, and it would make it easier for Congress to cut federal spending down the road.

3. Aid allocation does not match need. Supporters of federal grants assume that funding can be optimally distributed to those activities and states with the greatest needs. But even if such redistribution was a good idea, the aid system has never worked that way in practice. A July 1940 article in *Congressional Quarterly* lamented, "The grants-in-aid system in the United States has developed in a haphazard fashion. Particular services have been singled out for subsidy at the behest of pressure groups, and little attention has been given to national and state interests as a whole." And a June 1981 report by the Advisory Commission on Intergovernmental Relations concluded that "federal grant-in-aid programs have never reflected any consistent or coherent interpretation of national needs." The situation remains the same today. With highway aid, for example, some states with greater needs due to growing populations—such as Texas—consistently get the short end of the stick on funding.

4. Aid raises costs and reduces diversity. Federal grants reduce state diversity and innovation because they come with one-size-fits-all mandates. A good example was the 55-mile-per-hour national speed limit, which was enforced between 1974 and 1995 by federal threats of withdraw-

114

ing highway grant money. It never made sense that the same speed limit should be imposed in uncongested rural states and congested urban areas; Congress finally listened to motorists and repealed the mandate.

The Davis-Bacon labor rules are another example of harmful regulations tied to federal aid. State public works projects that receive federal aid must pay workers "prevailing wages." Since that generally means higher union-level wages, Davis-Bacon rules increase construction costs on government investments, such as highway projects.

5. Aid regulations breed bureaucracy. Federal aid is not a costless injection of funding to the states. Federal taxpayers pay the direct costs of the grants, but taxpayers at all levels of government are burdened by the costly bureaucracy needed to support the system. The aid system engulfs government workers with unproductive activities such as proposal writing, program reporting, regulatory compliance, auditing, and litigation.

Many of the 16 million people employed by state and local governments deal with the complex federal regulations attached to federal aid. There are specific sets of rules—sometimes hundreds of pages in length—for each of the more than 1,100 aid programs. There are also "crosscutting requirements," which are provisions that apply across federal aid programs, such as labor market rules.

6. Aid creates policymaker overload. One consequence of the large aid system is that the time spent by federal politicians on state and local issues takes away from their focus on truly national issues. Past investigations have revealed, for example, that most members of the House and Senate intelligence committees do not bother, or do not have the time, to read crucial intelligence reports. But members and their staff put great amounts of time and effort into steering spending toward their home states on local activities that should not have been federalized to begin with.

The federal involvement in hundreds of nonfederal policy areas overloads Washington's policy agenda. President Calvin Coolidge was right when he argued in 1925 that aid to the states should be cut because it was "encumbering the national government beyond its wisdom to comprehend, or its ability to administer" its proper roles.

7. Aid makes government responsibilities unclear. The three layers of government in the United States no longer resemble a tidy layer cake. Instead, they resemble a jumbled marble cake with responsibilities fragmented across multiple layers. Federal aid has made it difficult for citizens to understand which level of government is responsible for particular policies and activities. All three levels of government play big roles in such areas as transportation and education, which makes accountability difficult. After failures, politicians blame other levels of government, as was evident after Hurricane Katrina in 2005. When every level of government is responsible for a policy area, no level of government is responsible.

8. Common problems are not necessarily national priorities. Policymakers often argue that state, local, and private activities require federal intervention because they are "national priorities." But as President Reagan noted in Executive Order 12612, "It is important to recognize the distinction between problems of national scope (which may justify federal action) and problems that are merely common to the states (which will not justify federal action because individual states, acting individually or together, can effectively deal with them)."

Consider education. It is a high priority of local governments across the country and many millions of people, and thus there is no need for federal involvement. Federal involvement just creates bureaucracy and a national tug of war over funding. By contrast, when spending decisions are made at the local level, cost and benefit tradeoffs better reflect the preferences of people within each jurisdiction.

Conclusions

The federal aid system is a roundabout way of funding state and local activities. By federalizing those activities, we are asking Congress to do the impossible—to efficiently plan for the competing needs of a vast and diverse nation of 320 million people. The system thrives not because it creates good governance, but because it maximizes benefits to politicians. The system allows politicians at each level of government to take credit for spending, while blaming other levels of government for program failures and high tax burdens. The federal aid system is a triumph of expenditure without responsibility. It should be cut and eventually terminated altogether.

Suggested Readings

Edwards, Chris. "Federal Aid to the States: Historical Cause of Government Growth and Bureaucracy." Cato Institute Policy Analysis no. 593, May 22, 2007.
———. "Fiscal Federalism." DownsizingGovernment.org, Cato Institute, June 2013.

————. "Why the Federal Government Fails." Cato Institute Policy Analysis no. 777, July 27, 2015.

General Services Administration. *Catalog of Federal Domestic Assistance.* Washington: Government Printing Office, multiple years.

Office of Management and Budget. "Aid to State and Local Governments." *Budget of the United States Government, Fiscal Year 2017, Analytical Perspectives.* Washington: Government Printing Office, 2016.

Reagan, Ronald. Executive Order 12612, October 26, 1987.

—Prepared by Chris Edwards

13. Special-Interest Spending

When considering policy issues, federal lawmakers should have the broad public interest in mind. Unfortunately, that is not how the policy process often works in practice. Many programs are sustained by special-interest groups that gain narrow benefits at the expense of the general public. This chapter discusses why this occurs and focuses on one manifestation of the problem—business subsidies or "corporate welfare."

Special Interests Trump the General Interest

In an idealistic view of democracy, legislators always put average citizens first. They study alternatives, work toward a consensus, and pass legislation that has broad support. They also ensure that their actions are allowable under the U.S. Constitution.

The problem with this "public interest theory of government" is that it explains very little in the real world. Congress often enacts ill-conceived laws that benefit narrow groups at the expense of most citizens. Many federal programs harm the overall economy, and they are only sustained because interest groups support them.

Basic political incentives are to blame. To secure reelection, members of Congress try to gain the support of special-interest groups, particularly those that are important in their states. Members receive campaign support from interest groups and may even look forward to a post-congressional job with one of them. Furthermore, members get bombarded with seemingly convincing messages from interest groups about why subsidy programs are needed.

Members believe that they are doing the right thing when they support subsidies for their states or favored industries. What they don't seem to appreciate is that narrow subsidies nearly always make the nation as a whole worse off through higher taxes and economic distortions. The benefits created by subsidies are often visible and tangible, but the larger costs are diffused across millions of taxpayers or consumers.

Table 13.1
Majority Voting Does Not Ensure That Benefits Outweigh Costs

Legislator	Vote	Benefits Received by Constituents	Taxes Paid by Constituents
Sanders	Yea	$12	$10
Schumer	Yea	$12	$10
Shelby	Yea	$12	$10
Stabenow	Nay	$ 2	$10
Shaheen	Nay	$ 2	$10
Total	**Pass**	**$40**	**$50**

Table 13.1 shows how special-interest bills can gain majority support even if they are bad for the nation overall. A five-person legislature votes on a program that provides nationwide benefits of $40 but costs taxpayers $50. Assuming that legislators vote in the narrow interests of their states, the program garners a majority vote. The key to passage is that the benefits are more geographically concentrated than the costs. The legislation is a political success, but it is a failure for the nation because it costs more than it is worth.

Logrolling, or vote trading, makes special-interest provisions even easier to pass. Party leaders or committees bundle together many narrow provisions that benefit particular states and interest groups. Such bills often pass, even though the specific provisions do not have majority support on their own.

Table 13.2 shows how two subsidy programs can pass the five-person legislature, even though both have higher costs than benefits. Neither A nor B has majority support, and each would fail if voted on separately. So Sanders, Schumer, and Shelby agree to bundle the two programs in a single bill. They logroll. The two programs get approved, even though both of them impose a net cost on society.

Logrolling has been around since the 19th century. One early example was omnibus river and harbor bills, which sprinkled Army Corps of Engineers projects across many states to ensure passage. From the beginning, people observed that such bills included low-value projects that did not have broad support. In 1835, Tennessee Rep. Davy Crockett criticized the "log-roll" system, and in 1836, Virginia Rep. John Patton complained that a river and harbor bill being debated was a "species of log-rolling most disreputable and corrupting." In the early 20th century, scholar Chester Collins Maxey lambasted logrolling, arguing that it resulted in

Table 13.2
Logrolling Allows Passage of Narrow Subsidies

Legislator	Program A		Program B		Vote on Bill That Includes A and B
	Benefits Received by Constituents	Taxes Paid by Constituents	Benefits Received by Constituents	Taxes Paid by Constituents	
Sanders	$15	$10	$ 8	$10	Yea
Schumer	$15	$10	$ 8	$10	Yea
Shelby	$ 4	$10	$20	$10	Yea
Stabenow	$ 3	$10	$ 2	$10	Nay
Shaheen	$ 3	$10	$ 2	$10	Nay
Total	**$40**	**$50**	**$40**	**$50**	**Pass**

half the projects in omnibus bills, such as river and harbor bills, being "pure waste."

The magnitude of federal spending is much greater today, and so the logrolling problem is worse. Nearly all the spending in the $4 trillion budget stems from huge bills that bundle together many diverse provisions. Members have neither the time nor the incentive to rigorously critique individual programs in these large bills. So there is little debate about the real value of most federal spending.

Corporate Welfare

Corporate welfare is one manifestation of the special-interest spending problem. The budget contains many subsidies that aid some businesses at the expense of taxpayers and the overall economy. The government spends about $100 billion annually on corporate welfare, according to a 2012 Cato study. That amount includes direct grants and loans to companies, as well as indirect aid for industries.

Here are some of the corporate welfare programs in the federal budget:

- **Farm subsidies.** The U.S. Department of Agriculture (USDA) spends about $25 billion a year on an array of subsidies for farm businesses. Roughly a million farmers receive the subsidies, but the payments are tilted toward the largest producers. The largest 15 percent of farm businesses receive more than 85 percent of the subsidies. USDA data show that the average income of farm households was $119,880 in 2015, which was 51 percent higher than the average of all U.S. households.

- **Rural subsidies.** The USDA subsidizes rural businesses through the Rural Housing Service, the Rural Utilities Service, and the Rural Business-Cooperative Service. The programs, which cost about $4 billion a year, subsidize financial institutions, housing developers, utilities, and many other types of businesses—from car washes to clam harvesters.

- **Energy subsidies.** The Department of Energy spends more than $4 billion a year on subsidies for conventional and renewable energy. The subsidies include loans and grants to energy companies, and indirect business support such as industry research.

- **Small business subsidies.** The Small Business Administration provides subsidized loans and loan guarantees to businesses, which costs taxpayers about $800 million a year. Other federal agencies favor small businesses through preferential procurement rules and other methods.

- **Export subsidies.** The federal government provides aid to exporters through the Department of Commerce, the Foreign Military Financing program, and the Export-Import Bank. The latter agency provides loan guarantees and other aid to some of the nation's largest corporations, such as Boeing and General Electric.

- **Aviation subsidies.** The federal government spends billions of dollars a year on the operation of the air traffic control system and grants to commercial airports. But reforms in Canada and Great Britain show that airports and air traffic control can be separated from the government and self-funded.

- **Earned income tax credit (EITC).** The $70 billion EITC is usually thought of as a subsidy for low-income workers, but the program also subsidizes businesses. The EITC is designed to increase labor supply, but to the extent that it does, it reduces market wages for low-income workers. In effect, the program allows businesses to hire workers at a lower cost, with federal taxpayers picking up part of the wage bill.

This chapter focuses on spending for corporate welfare, but the government also subsidizes businesses through other means. International trade restrictions protect certain businesses at the expense of consumers and businesses that use imported goods. And in numerous industries, regulations protect established firms from competition by creating barriers to entry.

Another example of corporate welfare through regulation is the Renewable Fuel Standard, which requires that transportation fuels contain biofuel, primarily corn-based ethanol. The standard is a subsidy to corn farmers and the renewable fuels industry. It costs motorists about $10 billion a year, raises food prices, and does not benefit the environment.

What's Wrong with Corporate Welfare?

The above examples illustrate that corporate welfare comes in many flavors. "Crony capitalism" is another name for the problem. These subsidies have many negative effects:

1. They harm taxpayers. A 2012 Cato report found that the federal government spends about $100 billion annually on corporate welfare. Repealing the spending would save every household in the nation an average of about $800 a year.

2. They harm consumers and businesses. Corporate welfare aids some businesses, but it harms other businesses and consumers. Federal import barriers on sugar, for example, raise sugar prices and cost U.S. consumers about $2 billion a year. Some U.S. food companies that use sugar in their products have moved their production abroad to access lower-priced sugar.

3. They create an uneven playing field. Businesses receiving federal subsidies have an unfair advantage over unsubsidized competitors in their industries. Corporate welfare can also have unfair effects on businesses in other industries. As an example, the Export-Import program has subsidized jet purchases by foreign airlines, but that has given the foreign airlines an advantage over U.S. airlines that pay the full prices for their jets.

4. They duplicate private activities. Corporate welfare often duplicates activities that are already available in private markets, such as insurance, loans, marketing, and research. USDA's Risk Management Agency, for example, says that its mission is to help farm businesses "through effective, market-based risk management tools." But if these services are "market-based," then Congress can end this $8 billion agency and let the private marketplace provide the tools.

5. They foster corruption. Corporate welfare fosters political corruption as businesses looking for handouts try to gain the support of politicians and federal officials. A 2011 *Washington Post* investigation into green energy subsidies was titled, "Solyndra: Politics Infused Obama Energy Programs." The investigation found that the business people behind firms receiving green subsidies were often Obama campaign donors, that Solyndra's corporate decisionmaking was driven by political considerations, and that a major Democratic fundraiser and frequent visitor to the Obama White House, George Kaiser, held a one-third stake in Solyndra through his family foundation. Federal taxpayers lost half a billion dollars on the failed solar company, Solyndra.

6. They weaken the private sector. Corporate welfare draws talented people away from productive pursuits and into wasteful subsidy activities. Companies that take government subsidies often become weaker, less efficient, and distracted from serving their customers. They take on riskier projects, they make decisions divorced from market realities, and they substitute lobbying for innovation. Federal export subsidies, for example, induced Enron Corporation to partake in failed overseas projects that helped pull the company down. And in chasing federal green subsidies, the utility Southern Company has spent more than $6 billion on a disastrous "clean coal" power plant that has doubled in cost.

7. They damage trust in government and business. Public opinion polls show plunging support for politicians and big businesses over the years. Gallup polls find that just one-fifth of Americans have "confidence" in big business, and they find that about three-quarters of people think there is "widespread corruption" in American government. The recent rise of populist politicians partly stems from the feeling that the "system is rigged" in favor of special interests, such as big businesses. Business and political leaders would garner more respect if they cut their ties to each other by ending corporate welfare.

Conclusions

Corporate welfare and other special-interest subsidies should be abolished. But reforms will only happen if congressional leaders make it a priority and members of Congress understand that the nation would gain from overall restraint. In Washington, subsidies have grown in an environment where members perceive that it is "every man for himself" in securing favored spending.

Structural budget reforms would help Congress make tradeoffs. A balanced-budget requirement and a cap on the annual growth in total spending are mechanisms that would encourage restraint. Special commissions to downsize particular parts of the budget might also work, as they did with multiple rounds of military base closings.

Congress has the ability to end corporate welfare and other subsidy programs. But the job would be easier if Congress made structural reforms to limit special-interest pressures. It would also be made easier if more constituents pressured members to cut subsidies, particularly subsidies to members' own states.

Suggested Readings

Bennett, James T. *Corporate Welfare: Crony Capitalism That Enriches the Rich.* New Brunswick, NJ: Transaction Publishers, 2015.

Carney, Timothy. *The Big Ripoff: How Big Business and Big Government Steal Your Money.* New York: John Wiley & Sons, 2006.

Cato Institute. www.DownsizingGovernment.org.

Citizens Against Government Waste. www.cagw.org.

DeHaven, Tad. "Corporate Welfare in the Federal Budget." Cato Institute Policy Analysis no. 703, July 25, 2012.

Maxey, Chester Collins. "A Little History of Pork." *National Municipal Review* 8, no. 10 (December 1919): 691–705.

Taxpayers for Common Sense. www.taxpayer.net.

U.S. government spending database. www.usaspending.gov.

—*Prepared by Chris Edwards*

14. Fiscal Rules That Work

For the 2016 fiscal year, federal government spending reached an all-time high of almost $4 trillion. That means Washington consumed more than 21 percent of the economy's output. That's higher than the average of less than 19 percent of gross domestic product (GDP) between the end of World War II and 2008 and far above the average of less than 5 percent during America's first 150-plus years.

A rising burden of federal spending means ever-higher tax burdens and ever-larger amounts of government borrowing. A public sector that has grown too large is America's main fiscal challenge. A rising tax burden and growing levels of red ink are symptoms of the underlying disease of big government.

The Need for Long-Run Spending Restraint

Although budget numbers are grim today, the real challenge will be in the future. Because of an aging population and poorly designed entitlement programs, the federal government in the absence of reform is going to get much larger, redistributing greater and greater amounts of national income. The long-run fiscal outlook in the United States is just as bad as it is in many European welfare states. The only difference is that governments in those nations have a head start on the path to economic stagnation and fiscal crisis.

Figuring out how to restrain the growth of government spending is critically important. Fortunately, it shouldn't be that difficult. Even if the economy is weak, nominal economic output will expand by an average of about 4 percent annually (meaning about 2 percent "real" GDP growth). And that means about 4 percent to 5 percent more tax revenue every year. It's possible to slowly but surely control—and eventually shrink—the burden of federal spending if policymakers simply figure out some way to impose a spending cap so that outlays grow at a modest rate, say 2 percent annually.

Downsizing Federal Government Spending

Balanced Budget Rules Are Not Successful

When looking at rules to control federal spending, advocates of fiscal responsibility traditionally focused on some form of balanced budget amendment. A well-designed constitutional reform, restricting both red ink and the tax burden, would be a welcome change and could indirectly limit the size of the federal budget. But why focus on the symptom of red ink rather than the underlying problem of excessive spending? Shouldn't the real goal be to directly cap the growth of spending?

Looking at the states, 49 out of 50 have some sort of balanced budget requirement. Those rules have not protected states such as California, Illinois, and New Jersey from either bloated public sectors or large levels of debt. In the European Union, so-called Maastricht rules (also known as the Stability and Growth Pact) were imposed to prevent nations from having budget deficits of more than 3 percent of GDP and overall debt of more than 60 percent of GDP. These rules have not prevented unaffordable welfare states or rising levels of red ink in countries such as France, Italy, and Greece.

It might be possible to tighten these balanced budget rules and impose more effective restrictions on red ink, but that would be a major challenge, particularly in the United States. Constitutional reform here would require two-thirds support in both the House and Senate, followed by support from three-fourths of state legislatures. Given the poor track record of rules that attempt to restrict deficits, it would be better to focus on rules that seek to directly address the real problem of excessive government spending.

The Boom-Bust Cycle and Ratchet Effect

There's a very practical reason to focus on capping long-run spending rather than trying to balance the budget every year. Simply stated, the "business cycle" makes the latter very difficult.

There are two major determinants of tax revenue. The obvious one is the overall tax rate, but the size of the economy (i.e., the tax base) is equally relevant. A weak economy won't generate much additional tax revenue; a strong economy means that there are more wages to tax and more profits to tax. Thus, when a recession occurs and revenues drop, a balanced-budget mandate requires politicians to make dramatic changes at a time when they are especially reluctant to either raise taxes or impose spending restraint. Then, when the economy is enjoying strong growth and producing lots of tax revenue, a balanced-budget requirement doesn't impose much restraint on spending.

All of which creates an unfortunate cycle. Politicians spend a lot of money during the good years, creating expectations of more and more money for various interest groups. When a recession occurs, the politicians suddenly have to slam on the brakes. But even if they actually cut spending, it is rarely reduced to the level it was when the economy began its upswing. Moreover, politicians often raise taxes as part of these efforts to comply with anti-deficit rules. When the recession ends and revenues begin to rise again, the process starts over—this time from a higher base of spending and with a bigger tax burden. Over the long run, these cycles create a ratchet effect, with the burden of government spending always reaching new plateaus.

Spending Caps

Having some sort of rule to limit annual spending avoids the logistical problems of balanced-budget requirements. A spending cap tells politicians they can increase spending by, say, 2 percent when the economy is in recession. They like that better than a balanced-budget rule that would require actual cuts when revenue is dropping. But a spending cap also tells politicians they can increase spending by only 2 percent when the economy is growing quickly and revenues are rapidly increasing.

The challenge is to design an expenditure rule that works. There are many ways to design a spending cap, including reforms that would limit federal government spending to a certain share of overall economic output (18 percent of GDP, for instance). Scholars at the Mercatus Center have reviewed various rules and found that good results can be achieved with a simple approach that limits spending so it grows no faster than the population plus inflation:

> The effectiveness of [tax and expenditure limits (TELs)] varies greatly depending on their design. Effective TEL formulas limit spending to the sum of inflation plus population growth. This type of formula is associated with statistically significantly less spending. TELs tend to be more effective when they require a supermajority vote to be overridden, are constitutionally codified, and automatically refund surpluses. These rules are also more effective when they limit spending rather than revenue and when they prohibit unfunded mandates on local government. Having one or more of these characteristics tends to lead to less spending. Ineffective TELs are unfortunately the most common variety. TELs that tie state spending growth to growth in private income are associated with more spending in high-income states.

Professor Michael New reached a similar conclusion, pointing out that the relatively strict limits in Colorado have been especially effective.

> Why has Colorado's [Taxpayer's Bill of Rights] been more effective than other fiscal limits? . . . Colorado's Taxpayer's Bill of Rights . . . established a limit of inflation plus population growth. . . . [S]trong TELs have been able to restrict government growth. Holding other factors constant, strong TELs annually reduce growth in both state expenditures and state revenues by over $100 per capita.

The Swiss "debt brake," which functionally operates as a spending cap, has also been successful. It is described in a 2011 government report:

> The Swiss "debt brake" or "debt containment rule" . . . combines the stabilizing properties of an expenditure rule (because of the cyclical adjustment) with the effective debt-controlling properties of a balanced budget rule. . . . The amount of annual federal government expenditures has a cap, which is calculated as a function of revenues and the position of the economy in the business cycle. It is thus aimed at keeping total federal government expenditures relatively independent of cyclical variations.

One of the reasons the Swiss brake has been successful is that politicians are constrained from boosting spending during boom years when lots of tax revenue is generated.

> The debt-to-GDP ratio of the Swiss federal Government has decreased since the implementation of the debt brake in 2003. . . . In the past, economic booms tended to contribute to an increase in spending. . . . This has not been the case since the implementation of the fiscal rule, and budget surpluses have become commonplace. . . . The introduction of the debt brake has changed the budget process in such a way that the target for expenditures is defined at the beginning of the process, which must not exceed the ceiling provided by the fiscal rule. It has thus become a top-down process.

The Keynesian Case for Spending Caps

The underlying theory of Keynesian economics is that deficit spending should be increased during a recession to "prime the pump" of the economy. That theory doesn't make much sense since the government can't pour money into an economy unless it first borrows the money out of the economy.

That being said, a spending cap should appeal to Keynesians because it allows federal outlays to increase even during recession years when revenue is falling. Since Keynesians (at least in theory) claim to support surpluses during boom years, they should like the fact that a spending cap limits spending during those periods, thus ensuring that rising revenues will be used to reduce red ink.

Real-World Evidence

The bad news is that very few governments have imposed spending caps. The good news is that there have been very positive results when such policies are in effect. In Hong Kong, Article 107 of the Basic Law (the jurisdiction's constitution) states, "The Hong Kong Special Administrative Region shall . . . keep the budget commensurate with the growth rate of its gross domestic product." This sensible policy helps explain why total government spending averages less than 20 percent of GDP, significantly lower than the total burden of spending in America and far lower than in Europe's welfare states.

In Switzerland, voters used a referendum in 2001 to impose the aforementioned debt brake, which operationally functions as a spending cap. Outlays have expanded by only about 2 percent annually since the constitutional reform was implemented. That restraint has led to a modest reduction in the burden of spending relative to GDP and a big reduction in government debt as a share of economic output.

It is also noteworthy that Brazilian lawmakers amended the nation's constitution in late 2016 to impose a spending cap that freezes inflation-adjusted spending at current levels. Assuming the spending cap is enforced and there is some economic growth, that means the relative burden of government spending will shrink.

Even International Bureaucracies Agree

Surprisingly, even organizations such as the International Monetary Fund (IMF) and the Organization for Economic Cooperation and Development (OECD) have concluded that spending caps are the most effective type of fiscal rule. That development is rather remarkable given that these bureaucracies normally have a statist orientation on fiscal policy.

In February 2015, the IMF issued a very favorable assessment of spending caps:

[E]xpenditure rules have a better compliance record than budget balance and debt rules. . . . The higher compliance rate with expenditure rules is consistent with the fact that these rules are easy to monitor and that they immediately map into an enforceable mechanism—the annual budget itself. Besides, expenditure rules are most directly connected to instruments that the policymakers effectively control. By contrast, the budget balance, and even more so public debt, is more exposed to shocks, both positive and negative, out of the government's control.

Also important, a spending cap imposes discipline during boom years.

One of the desirable features of expenditure rules compared to other rules is that they are not only binding in bad but also in good economic times. . . . In contrast to other fiscal rules, countries also have incentives to break an expenditure rule in periods of high economic growth with increasing spending pressures. . . . [T]wo design features are in particular associated with higher compliance rates. . . . [C]ompliance is higher if the government directly controls the expenditure target. . . . Specific ceilings have the best performance record.

Another IMF study from March 2015 noted the problem of too much spending during years with robust revenue growth.

An analysis of stability programs during 1999–2007 suggests that actual expenditure growth in euro area countries often exceeded the planned pace, in particular when there were unanticipated revenue increases. Countries were simply unable to save the extra revenues and build up fiscal buffers. . . . This reveals an important asymmetry: governments were often unable to preserve revenue windfalls and faced difficulties in restraining their expenditure in response to revenue shortfalls when consolidation was needed. . . . The 3 percent of GDP nominal deficit ceiling did not prevent countries from spending their revenue windfalls in the mid-2000s. . . . Noncompliance has been the rule rather than the exception. . . . The drawbacks of the nominal deficit ceiling are particularly apparent when the economy is booming, as it is compatible with very large structural deficits.

So what's the solution? The report says spending caps work.

[T]he expenditure growth ceiling may seem the most appealing. This indicator is tractable (directly constraining the budget), easy to communicate to the public, and conceptually sound. . . . Based on simulations, Debrun and others (2008) show that an expenditure growth rule with a debt feedback ensures a better convergence towards the debt objective, while allowing greater flexibility in response to shocks. IMF (2012) demonstrates the good performance of the expenditure growth ceiling.

132

In July 2015, the OECD wrote:

[T]he adoption of a budget balance rule complemented by an expenditure rule could suit most countries well. . . . [T]he combination of the two rules responds to the two objectives. A budget balance rule encourages hitting the debt target. And, well-designed expenditure rules appear decisive in ensuring the effectiveness of a budget balance rule. Carnot (2014) shows also that a binding spending rule can promote fiscal discipline while allowing for stabilisation policies. . . . Spending rules entail no trade-off between minimising recession risks and minimising debt uncertainties. They can boost potential growth and hence reduce the recession risk without any adverse effect on debt. Indeed, estimations show that public spending restraint is associated with higher potential growth.

The OECD also addressed the issue in a November 2015 report. The highlights here include a warm embrace of the Swiss debt brake:

The European Union's Stability and Growth Pact . . . proved largely ineffective in protecting countries from the effects of the fiscal crisis. . . . Simple and clear fiscal anchors—e.g., the Swiss and German debt brake rules—appear to have been more effective in influencing effective fiscal management. . . . A combination of a budget balance rule and an expenditure rule seems to suit most countries well. . . . [W]ell-designed expenditure rules appear decisive to ensure the effectiveness of a budget balance rule and can foster long-term growth. . . . Spending rules entail no trade-off between minimising recession risks and minimising debt uncertainties. They can boost potential growth and hence reduce the recession risk without any adverse effect on debt. Indeed, estimations show that public spending restraint is associated with higher potential growth.

In December 2015, the European Central Bank issued a report on fiscal rules. A key point was that deficit-oriented rules don't bind politicians during growth years: "[D]uring a boom phase, fiscal rules do not prevent fiscal policy from turning expansionary." Once again, spending caps got the highest marks.

Regarding the different types of fiscal rules, we find particularly strong coefficients for expenditure rules, possibly reflecting the fact that expenditure rules are easier to monitor and are thereby more credible. . . . If a country had a fiscal rule in place for the past ten years, the average fiscal space for those years is around 22% of GDP higher. The coefficient is proportional to the number of years in which a fiscal rule has been in place. . . . [I]f governments have fiscal rules in place, the results suggest that governments can no longer fully use their fiscal space and (on average) are even forced to reduce their current expenditures. . . . [E]xpenditure rules . . . are correlated with a lower coefficient for fiscal space on procyclicality. This is in line with our findings . . . that expenditure rules might restrict discretionary expenditures.

Conclusion

When even the IMF and OECD agree that spending caps are effective, that's a remarkable sign that all other options do *not* work. But there really wasn't any other possible conclusion. Requirements for balanced budgets in 49 out of 50 states haven't prevented wasteful spending and more debt. Maastricht anti-deficit and anti-debt rules in the European Union haven't blocked bloated welfare states and fiscal crisis.

Spending caps are simple and easy to understand, and they directly address the real problem of excessive spending. And in the few places they've been tried, the evidence shows that dealing with the underlying disease of too much government automatically fixes the symptom of red ink. The United States could avert a very bad long-run fiscal crisis by copying the wise policies of Switzerland and Hong Kong.

Suggested Readings

Mitchell, Daniel J. "A Big Fiscal Victory: Constitutional Spending Caps for Brazil!" *International Liberty*, December 15, 2016.

———. "America's Greek Fiscal Future." *Cato at Liberty*, June 19, 2015.

———. "Balanced Budget Requirements Don't Work as Well as Spending Limits." *Cato at Liberty*, May 26, 2015.

———. "By the Numbers: America's Unfortunate Fiscal Evolution from Madisonian Constitutionalism to Wilsonian Statism." *Cato at Liberty*, September 14, 2015.

———. "Even the IMF Agrees that Spending Caps Are Effective." *Cato at Liberty*, March 16, 2015.

———. "Hong Kong's Remarkable Fiscal Policy." *International Liberty*, October 14, 2014.

———. "If You Want Good Fiscal Policy, Forget the Balanced Budget Amendment and Pursue Spending Caps." *Cato at Liberty*, March 2, 2015.

———. "Maintaining and Enforcing Spending Caps Is a Huge Test of GOP Credibility on Fiscal Policy." *Cato at Liberty*, August 11, 2015.

———. "Proven Reforms to Restrain Leviathan." *Cato at Liberty*, May 28, 2015.

———. "The Simple Solution to America's Deteriorating Fiscal Outlook." *Cato at Liberty*, January 26, 2016.

———. "The Six Most Important Takeaways from CBO's New Long-Run Fiscal Forecast." *Cato at Liberty*, July 13, 2016.

———. "A Swiss-Style Spending Cap Would Have Prevented the Current Fiscal Mess in America." *International Liberty*, December 20, 2012.

———. "Switzerland's 'Debt Brake' Is a Role Model for Spending Control and Fiscal Restraint." *International Liberty*, April 26, 2012.

—Prepared by Daniel J. Mitchell

15. Averting National Bankruptcy

The United States federal government debt is on an unsustainable path; that is, the government is in (extreme) fiscal imbalance. In particular, the four main entitlement programs (Medicare, Medicaid, Obamacare, and Social Security) are collectively growing far faster than any plausible path for gross domestic product (GDP). Congress should curtail these programs to avoid fiscal Armageddon.

Background

The United States faces a challenging fiscal future. According to projections from the Congressional Budget Office (CBO), the debt-to-GDP ratio will hit at least 181 percent by 2090 and continue to climb unless the nation adjusts its tax and spending policies. If no policy changes occur and the debt ratio continues on its projected path for an extended period, the United States will eventually face rising interest rates on its debt, an even steeper debt path, and a fiscal crisis. This outcome is not inevitable; the United States likely has decades to adjust its policies. Few dispute, however, that unless the CBO's projections are substantially too pessimistic, the United States needs major adjustments in spending or tax policies to avoid fiscal meltdown.

Despite widespread agreement that spending or tax policies must change, however, appropriate adjustments have so far not occurred. Indeed, many recent policy changes have worsened the U.S. fiscal situation. These include the creation of Medicare Part D ($65 billion in 2014); new subsidies under the Affordable Care Act, often called Obamacare ($13.7 billion in 2014); the expansion of Medicaid under Obamacare (from $250.9 billion in 2009 to $301.5 billion in 2014); higher defense spending (from $348.46 billion in 2002 to $603.46 billion in 2014); increased spending on veterans' benefits and services (from $70.4 billion in 2006 to $161.2 billion in 2014); and greater spending on energy programs (average annual spending rose from $0.52 billion over 1998–2002 to $11.43 billion over

2010–2014). Politicians across the spectrum, moreover, propose additional spending all the time.

"Fiscal imbalance" is the excess of what we expect to spend, including repayment of our debt, over what government expects to receive in revenue. A plausible explanation for America's failure to address its fiscal imbalance is a belief that "this time is no different," since earlier alarms have not ended in fiscal meltdown. In the 1980s, for example, the government experienced a large buildup of federal debt due to President Ronald Reagan's tax cuts and increases in military spending. Concern arose over the spiraling debt, causing congressional budget showdowns during President Bill Clinton's first term. But, ultimately, no serious fiscal crisis ensued.

In 2011, fears of a U.S. government default arose during the debt-ceiling crisis. Disagreements between members of Congress resulted in a political stalemate, massive public apprehension, and a one-notch downgrade of the U.S. credit rating. Just before the deadline, however, the Budget Control Act was signed into law, raising the debt ceiling by more than $2.1 trillion and staving off the threat of immediate default. A similar crisis loomed in 2013 when Congress's inability to rein in the federal deficit almost triggered a "fiscal cliff"—a series of deep, automatic cuts to federal spending. Once again, with only hours to spare, lawmakers reached a compromise and averted larger economic consequences. Overall, the past 30 years reveal a clear trend: time and time again, alarm erupts over the rising federal debt level, but full fiscal meltdown never materializes. Thus, many people dismiss claims that U.S. fiscal balance is a calamity in waiting, believing "this time is no different."

In truth, this time *is* different. Although fiscal meltdown is not imminent, the nation's fiscal situation has been deteriorating since the mid-1960s, is far worse than ever before, and will get worse as time passes and no adjustments occur. This view follows from looking not just at current deficits and the current value of the debt; these are incomplete measures of the government's fiscal situation because they account only for past expenditure relative to tax revenue. The true impact of existing expenditure and tax policies depends as well on the projected paths of future expenditure and tax revenues. The standard measure of the overall fiscal situation is known as fiscal imbalance, which adds up (in a way that adjusts for interest rates) all future expenditures, minus future tax revenues, plus the explicit debt.

Figure 15.1 presents estimates of U.S. fiscal imbalance for the period 1965–2014. Imbalance has risen enormously from roughly zero in 1965 to $118 trillion in 2014, which is roughly seven times current GDP.

Figure 15.1
Projected Fiscal Imbalance, 1965–2014

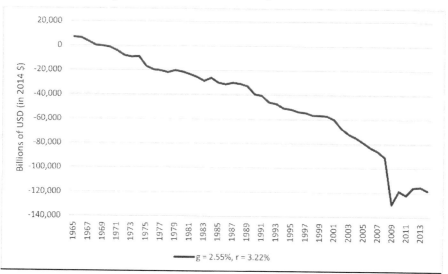

NOTE: The estimates assume an average annual GDP growth rate (g) of 2.55 percent and real interest rate (r) of 3.22 percent, which reflect median growth and average interest rates over the past 40 years.

SOURCE: Jeffrey Miron, *U.S. Fiscal Imbalance over Time: This Time Is Different.* Washington: Cato Institute, 2016.

The reason for the persistent decline in fiscal balance is that the composition of federal expenditure has shifted markedly since 1965, especially from defense spending to mandatory health and retirement spending—that is, entitlements. Defense spending has declined relative to GDP over the post-WWII period; this spending could increase in the future but is unlikely to grow without bound. Entitlement spending, however, not only consumes a large fraction of the federal budget, it is also likely to grow faster than GDP, indefinitely, under current law. This excess growth reflects the increasing share of the population collecting benefits relative to younger people paying taxes, as well as the impact of subsidized health insurance on health care cost inflation. Thus, CBO forecasts that health and retirement spending will increase substantially faster than GDP going forward.

In principle, the United States has three options for restoring fiscal balance: faster economic growth, higher taxes, or slower expenditure growth. In practice, only slower growth of entitlement spending can make a significant difference. Even if economic growth achieved its highest

137

historical levels, that would not alter imbalance materially. Similarly, even if taxes were raised substantially above their postwar average—and had no adverse effect on growth—fiscal imbalance would still be large.

That leaves expenditure cuts as the only viable way to significantly reduce fiscal imbalance. And the cuts must target entitlements, since those programs are large and are the ones growing relative to GDP. The crucial difference between expenditure cuts and tax hikes is that the former could plausibly increase growth, by reducing distortions in health and retirement decisions, while the latter would almost certainly reduce growth, making imbalance worse. Thus, cutting the growth of federal health and retirement expenditure is a win-win. Congress has three main options for cutting entitlements and averting bankruptcy.

Raise the Eligibility Age for Social Security and Medicare

The original justification for Social Security and Medicare was to help citizens who could no longer care for themselves. When Congress created Social Security in 1935, life expectancy was 63 and the age of eligibility was 65, so Social Security was insurance against "living too long." Similarly, when Congress adopted Medicare in 1965, life expectancy was about 70 and the age of eligibility was again 65, so most beneficiaries expected only a few years of subsidized health care. Today's average life expectancy, however, has reached nearly 79. Social Security's age of "normal retirement" has increased by only two years since 1965, and Medicare's is still 65. Unsurprisingly, the total number of Social Security beneficiaries has skyrocketed; 25 million Americans received Social Security benefits in 1970, compared with 60 million in 2015.

Thus, as life expectancy has steadily increased, and health conditional on age has improved, Social Security and Medicare have evolved from helping only those in serious need to also providing income support and subsidized health insurance, over decades, for middle- and upper-income households. Simultaneously, the fraction of the population receiving benefits has grown relative to the fraction paying taxes, making these programs fiscally unsustainable. Thus, under current parameters, both programs have grown far beyond their original intent and have become unaffordable.

Congress should raise the age of eligibility in both programs, by at least enough to offset the increase in life expectancy since creation of the programs. The higher ages could be phased in gradually, for example, by six months every year for some number of years, with the higher age affecting only those below some cutoff, such as age 50. Thus, the higher eligibility ages would not affect those already receiving benefits or even those within 15 years of (current) eligibility. Congress should also index the eligibility age to future increases in life expectancy; this would avoid future expansions of Social Security and Medicare relative to the size of the economy.

Increase Deductibles and Copayments for Medicare, Obamacare, and Medicaid

Standard economics explains that people demand health insurance to protect themselves financially in the case of major illnesses or accidents, not to cover routine expenditures such as for checkups, medications, and other moderate and predictable outlays. This implies that economically efficient health insurance should have substantial deductibles.

Standard economics also suggests that economically efficient health insurance should come with significant copays. Insurance can generate excessive health expenditure because the insured do not pay the costs of their care (a phenomenon known as moral hazard). One remedy is deductibles; a second is copays, the portion of health expenditure paid by the insured person, after the deductible has been met. Copays do not fully balance the costs of care against the benefits, but they nudge health care decisions in the right direction while still reducing the risk of large outlays for the insured.

Thus, Congress should modify Medicare, Obamacare, and Medicaid to incorporate significantly higher deductibles and copays. The appropriate adjustments differ across programs, but increases of at least 50 to 100 percent, or more, make sense in many cases. For example, the yearly deductible for Medicare Part A is only $1,288 and for most Part B benefits, only $166. Obamacare caps yearly out-of-pocket spending for deductibles and copays at $6,850 for self-only coverage and $13,700 for family coverage. Medicaid charges minimal copays for those below 150 percent of the federal poverty level.

Freeze (Real) Social Security Benefits

Under current policy, the level of Social Security benefits that an individual receives is a function of that individual's earnings history. In market economies, wages tend to rise with worker productivity (which in turn reflects technological progress); so as an economy experiences productivity growth, real wages rise. Thus, the inflation-adjusted level of Social Security benefits grows along with the economy's increase in overall productivity. Indeed, over the past four decades, the average annual Social Security benefit (in real terms) has more than doubled, from $7,200 per recipient in 1970 to $14,900 in 2015 (constant 2015 dollars).

Assuming Social Security exists to prevent poverty, the ongoing increase in benefit levels is excessive. Instead, society should determine a level of benefits that allows those without other income to attain some modest standard of living; Congress should keep that level in place over time.

Congress should therefore freeze the level of real benefits at its current value; this amounts to indexing the level of new benefits to price rather than wage inflation. Under this approach, Social Security expenditure would grow far more slowly than under the current system because it would only reflect increases in the population age 65 and over, rather than also increasing with productivity.

Suggested Readings

Gokhale, Jagadeesh. "Spending Beyond Our Means: How We Are Bankrupting Future Generations." Cato Institute White Paper, February 13, 2013.

Miron, Jeffrey. "Curtailing Subsidies for Health Insurance." In *Reviving Economic Growth*, edited by Brink Lindsey. Washington: Cato Institute, 2015.

———. *Fiscal Imbalance: A Primer.* Washington: Cato Institute, 2015.

———. *U.S. Fiscal Imbalance over Time: This Time Is Different,* Washington: Cato Institute, 2016.

—Prepared by Jeffrey Miron

Contributors

Michael F. Cannon is the Cato Institute's director of health policy studies, coeditor of *Replacing Obamacare: The Cato Institute on Health Care Reform*, and coauthor of *Healthy Competition: What's Holding Back Health Care and How to Free It.*

Chris Edwards is director of tax policy studies at the Cato Institute, editor of DownsizingGovernment.org, and coauthor of *Global Tax Revolution: The Rise of Tax Competition and the Battle to Defend It.*

Benjamin H. Friedman is a former research fellow in defense and homeland security studies at the Cato Institute.

Neal McCluskey is director of the Cato Institute's Center for Educational Freedom and author of *Feds in the Classroom: How Big Government Corrupts, Cripples, and Compromises American Education.*

Jeffrey Miron is director of economic studies at the Cato Institute, director of undergraduate studies in the Department of Economics at Harvard University, and author of *Libertarianism from A to Z.*

Daniel J. Mitchell is a former senior fellow at the Cato Institute and coauthor of *Global Tax Revolution: The Rise of Tax Competition and the Battle to Defend It.*

Michael D. Tanner is a senior fellow at the Cato Institute, author of *Going for Broke: Deficits, Debt, and the Entitlement Crisis* and *The Poverty of Welfare: Helping Others in Civil Society*, and coauthor of *A New Deal for Social Security.*

Ian Vásquez is director of the Cato Institute's Center for Global Liberty and Prosperity, coauthor of *The Human Freedom Index*, and editor of *Global Fortune: The Stumble and Rise of World Capitalism.*

Cato Institute

Founded in 1977, the Cato Institute is a public policy research foundation dedicated to broadening the parameters of policy debate to allow consideration of more options that are consistent with the principles of limited government, individual liberty, and peace. To that end, the Institute strives to achieve greater involvement of the intelligent, concerned lay public in questions of policy and the proper role of government.

The Institute is named for Cato's Letters, libertarian pamphlets that were widely read in the American Colonies in the early 18th century and played a major role in laying the philosophical foundation for the American Revolution.

Despite the achievement of the nation's Founders, today virtually no aspect of life is free from government encroachment. A pervasive intolerance for individual rights is shown by government's arbitrary intrusions into private economic transactions and its disregard for civil liberties. And while freedom around the globe has notably increased in the past several decades, many countries have moved in the opposite direction, and most governments still do not respect or safeguard the wide range of civil and economic liberties.

To address those issues, the Cato Institute undertakes an extensive publications program on the complete spectrum of policy issues. Books, monographs, and shorter studies are commissioned to examine the federal budget, Social Security, regulation, military spending, international trade, and myriad other issues. Major policy conferences are held throughout the year, from which papers are published thrice yearly in the *Cato Journal*. The Institute also publishes the quarterly magazine *Regulation*.

In order to maintain its independence, the Cato Institute accepts no government funding. Contributions are received from foundations, corporations, and individuals, and other revenue is generated from the sale of publications. The Institute is a nonprofit, tax-exempt, educational foundation under Section 501(c)3 of the Internal Revenue Code.

CATO INSTITUTE
1000 Massachusetts Ave., N.W.
Washington, D.C. 20001
www.cato.org